Finding Your Way
As a Counselor

Jeffrey A. Kottler

Editor

ACA

AMERICAN
COUNSELING
ASSOCIATION

FINDING YOUR WAY AS A COUNSELOR

10 9 8 7 6 5 4 3

American Counseling Association
5999 Stevenson Avenue
Alexandria, VA 22304

Acquisitions and Development Editor
Carolyn Baker

Managing Editor
Michael Comlish

Cover design by Jennifer Sterling, Spot Color
Cover art by Lane Vance

Library of Congress Cataloging-in-Publication Data

American Counseling Association
    Finding your way as a counselor / Jeffrey A. Kottler, editor.
      p. cm.
    Includes bibliographical references (p.   ).
    ISBN 1-55620-161-3 (alk. paper)
      1. Counselors. 2. Counseling. I. Kottler, Jeffrey A.
BF637.C6F377 1997
158'.3—dc20

96-9282
CIP

TABLE OF CONTENTS

PART VI- RECOGNITION AND SELF-PROMOTION

PART VII- TRANSITIONS AND TRANSFORMATIONS

PART VIII- REACHING OUT

About the Editor

Jeffrey A. Kottler began the column "Finding Your Way" in 1992 as a way to address some of the most difficult challenges that counselors face. He is a professor in the Department of Counseling and Educational Psychology at the University of Nevada, Las Vegas. Jeffrey has authored or co-authored over 20 books in the fields of counseling, psychology, and education, including: *On Being a Therapist, Introduction to Therapeutic Counseling, The Emerging Professional Counselor, Growing a Therapist,* and *The Language of Tears.*

ABOUT THE AUTHORS

Myrna B. Alexander is the regional manager for an employee assistance program for AT&T. In addition, she maintains a private counseling, employee assistance and mental health consultation practice in Arlington, Virginia.

Brent Bandhauer is an elementary school counselor in Las Vegas, Nevada.

Fred Bemak is an Associate Professor and Chair of the Department of Counseling and Human Services at Johns Hopkins University, Baltimore, Maryland.

Diane Blau is a retired counselor and counselor educator living in Santa Barbara, California.

Jesse Brinson is an Associate Professor of counseling and educational psychology at the University of Nevada, Las Vegas, specializing in multicultural issues and substance abuse counseling.

Laurie Carty is a counselor and nurse educator at the University of Windsor, Ontario.

Gerald Corey is a Professor of counseling at California State University, Fullerton.

Toni DiMargio is a counselor at Churchill Counseling Services in Youngstown, Ohio.

Shirley Emerson is President of the State of Nevada Board of Marriage and Family Therapist Examiners.

Alan W. Forrest is an Associate Professor of Counselor Education at Radford University, Radford, Virginia.

Holly Forester-Miller is an Associate Professor of counseling at West Virginia Graduate College, Institute, West Virginia.

Samuel T. Gladding is Professor of Counseling at Wake Forest University, Winston-Salem, North Carolina.

Mark R. Gover is a counselor at the CONCERN Employee Assistance Program in Lansing, Michigan.

April Peck Herbert is Associate Director of the Peace Corps in Manila, Philippines.

IX

Paul Jones is Chair and Professor of counseling and educational psychology at the University of Nevada, Las Vegas, where he specializes in assistive technology for persons with disabilities.

Meetu Khosla is a counselor working at Jeewan (Mala) Hospital in New Delhi, India.

Jeffrey A. Kottler is a Professor of counseling and educational psychology at the University of Nevada, Las Vegas.

Wayne Lanning is a Professor of counseling and educational psychology at the University of Nevada, Las Vegas.

Deborah Linnell works on an elite team of retired police officers with the National Center for Missing and Exploited Children to assist families and law enforcement personnel search for missing children.

Wendy Lee Logan is a counselor at Erwin Middle School in Asheville, North Carolina.

Don Martin is Associate Dean at Regent University, Virginia Beach, Virginia.

Garrett J. McAuliffe is an Associate Professor of counseling at Old Dominion University, Norfolk, Virginia.

Melinda Lewis Merrigan is a counselor at Mount Lebanon Elementary School, West Lebanon, New Hampshire.

Jay Noricks lives and counsels in Las Vegas, Nevada.

Vicky Phillips is President of Lifelong Learning and Director of Counseling with the Electronic University Network on America Online.

Shan Pincus is a mental health counselor in Teaneck, New Jersey specializing in the addictive personality.

Kathy Potter is a counselor in Albuquerque, New Mexico.

Mark Schorr works as a counselor at Network Behavioral HealthCare in Portland, Oregon.

Marie M. Schrader is a counselor in private practice and adjunct faculty member at the University of Nevada, Las Vegas.

Stuart Sobel is a retired Supervisor of Guidance for the Brooklyn/Staten Island senior high schools.

Mark E. Young is Associate Professor and Chair of the Counseling Department of Stetson University, DeLand, Florida.

PREFACE

During the past several years, the "Finding Your Way" column in *Counseling Today* has been among the most widely read and best loved features of the American Counseling Association newsletter. Readers have appreciated both the quality of the writing and the poignancy of the personal stories in which counselors have spoken honestly about their foibles, doubts, failures, vulnerabilities, joys and successes.

Addressed originally to beginners in the field trying to find their way through a maze of confusion and challenges, experienced practitioners as well have found wisdom and inspiration in the essays covering a wide range of themes that have rarely been discussed: hypocrisy, fear of failure, professional dysfunction, spirituality and the like. The pieces are written in a style that is both engaging and provocative.

This book is a collection of the best pieces that have appeared throughout the years—they are most insightful in the sense that they describe some of the realities involved in counseling practice that have often been ignored. Some of the contributors are well-known authors. Many of them, however, are first-time writers who struggled mightily through four or five different attempts to put their thoughts and feelings into words.

WHO THIS BOOK IS FOR

This book would be of interest to counseling practitioners in a variety of settings. The essays address issues in school, mental health, private practice, military, university and industrial settings, as well as themes that are relevant to all professionals.

Throughout the years, many counselor educators have been copying the articles for use in their classes. This book also has appeal as a supplementary text in a variety of counseling courses from introduction and orientation classes to counseling seminars at the masters and doctoral level.

What all of these essays have in common is that they come from the heart. They speak the truth. They are profoundly personal statements about what it means to find your way as a counselor. It is my hope that others can learn from our stories, and find strength in their inspirational messages.

CONTENTS OF THE BOOK

This collection of essays is organized according to several broad themes. We begin with a series of essays in which the authors speak honestly and sincerely about their own doubts and insecurities. Although our clients and the public expect, if not demand, that we show a degree of confidence in our healing powers that we don't often feel, much of the time we have far less to offer others than we would prefer. The authors in this section, many of whom are just starting out their careers, wonder when they will ever feel like real counselors. The section ends with a number of veterans, as well, reminiscing about what it was like for them to be a newcomer to this strange and wonderful profession.

In Part II, Feeling Lost, we continue the exploration of the ways counselors struggle with their confusion. Each of the authors discusses times in which there was a pervasive feeling of not knowing enough, or not being able to do enough to be helpful.

The third section focuses on those times when counselors face themselves. The authors demonstrate courage and openness talking about their awareness of feeling wounded during times when they are dealing with other people's pain. They speak about coming to terms with their own emotional vulnerabilities, and their subsequent attempts to face their own unresolved issues.

Part IV, Making A Difference, is considerably more upbeat. After all, finding our way in this profession isn't just about dealing with our limitations, but also coming to terms with the opportunities to help those who need it most. The authors discuss how they came to terms with their own sense of potency as helpers, even when working with some people who really challenged them.

The fifth section, Refining Our Thinking, continues exploration of the ways counselors have grown and evolved in their development. A number of authors speak about how they have continued to reflect on the meaning of their work, how they have personalized and developed considerably what they once learned in graduate school and read in books. Finding your way as a counselor means, in part, integrating all you have learned, not only from your teachers and supervisors, but from your clients. The authors talk about how they have developed their own theories regarding how counseling works, how to plan for maximum therapeutic impact, and how to make mature ethical decisions.

In Part VI, we hear success stories of a few practitioners who talk about how they have come to terms with their image in the eyes of their clients. Recognition and self-promotion are a necessary part of developing credibility among the population of folks we might serve.

The seventh section is about transition and transformation of the counselor. A number of authors tell the stories of how they found their way into the field from a number of other professions. They talk about how they used the background from their previous lives to create a unique image of themselves as counselors. A few other contributors discuss how they have continued to grow and evolve much later in their careers as a result of life transitions.

The book closes by moving from the inward to the outward. In the last section, the authors talk about how critical it is for counselors to reach out and support one another. Counseling can be such lonely and isolating work. Finding our way in this profession is not a journey that can be taken alone; it requires the stimulation of mentors and supervisors, as well as the nurturance and guidance of our friends, family and colleagues. The book ends on a note of encouraging readers to be their own mentors as well, to take responsibility for their own continued growth and development just as we do for our clients.

Jeffrey A. Kottler
Las Vegas, Nevada

PART I

In the
Beginning

CHAPTER 1

FINDING YOUR WAY
AS A COUNSELOR

Jeffrey A. Kottler

Although the original intent of these essays was to speak directly to beginners in the field, many topics are also relevant for veteran counselors, especially those who have close contact with beginning counselors. Those of us who are supervisors, or who mentor new professionals, understand that one of the major benefits of our work is that it encourages us to continuously examine the same issues that beginners grapple with. These struggles include, but are not limited to, the following themes that will be explored in this book:

Grieving the loss of graduate school—Although you might feel relieved at finally having escaped the rigors of academic life—the pressure, evaluations, exams, papers, tuition bills, classes—there is also a feeling of loss because the structure for learning is gone. Many new graduates talk about the freedom and independence they now feel, but also about how much they miss their classmates, the stimulation from intellectual dialogue, the intensive supervision and the guidance of their mentors.

Recruiting a new mentor—What beginning counselors (and *all* practitioners) need most is someone they can rely on to help them learn the ropes. We need this mentor to help us process cases and work with countertransference issues, as well as advocating for us within our organization. A mentor is absolutely critical to help any professional, but especially a beginner, navigate the maze of political and practical realities that they never faced in graduate school.

Creating a new support system—A benevolent and wise supervisor is certainly a requirement for job satisfaction, but so is peer support. Many of us chose this profession because we are "people oriented"; we like interacting with others, especially those who share similar values and interests. If such a group of cohorts is not available in your workplace, then you should find and recruit individuals who can support you, understand and respond to your professional and personal needs, and generally help you to revitalize yourself after especially grueling days or weeks.

Trying to do too much—As a beginner in the field, you have a lot to prove—to yourself and to your peers. One of the most common mistakes made by those starting out (as well as many veterans) is taking too much responsibility for client progress. When a client does not cooperate or does not wish to change according to our preferred schedule, a beginner often tries to jump in and rescue, to work even harder. The assumption is: "If only I knew more, or I were more skilled, or better trained, or smarter, or more sensitive, or if I pushed just a little harder, then surely this client would come around." Of course the reality is that sometimes when we try to do too much or take too active a role in counseling, we make it even easier for the client to avoid responsibility for what happens.

Refining a model for practice—One of the first things new counselors learn upon entering the workforce (or their internships) is that single-theory allegiance is more an academic exercise than a pragmatic reality. A lot of flexibility is required on a daily basis for us to reach a diverse constituency. One of the major challenges for beginners and veterans alike is to continually revise and evolve our models of practice as we learn new things and are exposed to new ideas.

Playing catch-up with things you should have learned—"Didn't they teach you *anything* in school?" is a frequent lament by colleagues who have been in the field for a while and who feel impatient with the beginner's struggle to fill in knowledge and skill gaps. No matter how comprehensive your training was, every professional position has its own unique demands that could not have been anticipated or planned for.

Challenging your ethical reasoning—You memorized the *ACA Code of Ethics and Standards of Practice.* Your copy of the *ACA Ethical Standards Casebook,* Fifth Edition is dogeared from overuse. But now you are alone. A grateful client offers you a gift; should you accept it? A client asks if it is all right if you go for a walk together instead of staying cooped up in the office. Does that constitute a boundary issue? Is it a dual relationship if you write a letter of reference for an ex-client?

There are no simple answers to many ethical questions. Often there is very little time to consult with a colleague or supervisor before you have to make a decision. Now is the moment of truth—when you find out if you have really mastered the principles of ethical reasoning that you learned in school.

Maintaining a positive attitude in the face of cynicism—New practitioners often have unbridled enthusiasm for what they are doing. This idealism sometimes stands in marked contrast to more experienced counselors who have been in the field for some time and may have developed attitudes of cynicism or even burnout. It is challenging to control one's unrealistic expectations for what is possible without sacrificing excitement in the process.

Dealing with fears of failure—While students struggle with issues related to whether they have what it takes to be an effective counselor, new graduates are more concerned with other themes: "What if I don't know what to do with a particular client?"; "What if I make a mistake and harm somebody irrevocably?"; "What if I make a fool out of myself and my supervisor finds out?"; "What if my colleagues discover that I really don't know what I am doing most of the time?"

As you progress in your professional development, the struggles with your fears of failure don't stop—the questions just become more difficult. A veteran, for example, is wrestling with self-queries such as, "What if I am not really doing anything, if counseling is all a sham?" or "What if my life's work really doesn't matter, if all my devotion and commitment don't make much of a difference in the world?"

In time, of course, both beginners and experienced practitioners alike learn that failure becomes the teacher that promotes greater humility, reflection, flexibility and experimentation. Through our mistakes and misjudgments we become most aware of what is least helpful to others. This feedback is just as useful as the most glowing reports of our successes.

In the chapters that follow, each of these themes will be developed further through the voices of several dozen practitioners representing different counseling specialties, settings, and stages in professional development. We sincerely hope these stories help you to find your own way as a counselor.

CHAPTER 2

WAITING FOR WISDOM TO ARRIVE

Brent Bandhauer

I have been finding my way as a school counselor in two different elementary schools for a little more than a year now. I love going to work because it feels great to have these students enthusiastically greet me whenever I appear on the playground or in the halls. I feel like a celebrity when I go to conduct a class guidance lesson and the students cheer because I've arrived. I feel proud when teachers ask me about how they can begin their own careers as school counselors.

The problem, however, is that even after having graduated from an accredited master's program, I didn't learn nearly enough to actually be a school counselor. I sometimes wonder if I really paid enough attention in class or if I read my text books too casually. Maybe I just forgot the important concepts that I need to be a helper of children. Yet if I'm asked, I can glibly explain the core conditions necessary for change. I can give a mini-lecture on irrational beliefs and how they impair daily functioning. I can even describe outcome research studies that begin to pinpoint the actual reasons clients do change. Perhaps I studied the theories with the assumption I would be helping insightful clients who know what changes they want. Does the source of this problem lie in my personal shortcomings or in my training?

To answer this question, I decided to keep track of and identify the antecedents to my feelings of inadequacy. The first clue was discovered when a child told me that her mom abruptly left the family. I could see her distress and made a beautiful empathic response, "Ah, you feel confused and deeply hurt because your mom hasn't even given you an explanation about her leaving." The door was opened to delve into deeper self-disclosure. Her response? "Yeah." I let the silence hang for her to process what she was feeling. Suddenly she looked at me with confusion about why I was just sitting there. I restated the reflection using different words in case my empathic terminology was too abstract. "Yeah," she responded again. I finished the session by helping her identify the coping skills she had already put to use. My empathic concern gave her comfort but I'm not sure I guided her toward maturity and personal development.

Soon, I identified another reason I feel unprepared. Before school one morning, a student begged me to talk to her because she desperately needed help. During the session, I quickly discovered that she really had nothing important to talk about. She just wanted out of class. I carefully explained to her that counseling was for people who were experiencing concerns they didn't know what to do about. Then I began to wonder how many other sessions I had spent with students who really just wanted entertainment.

These feelings of being under-trained began appearing everywhere. I'm often called upon to participate as a team member with teachers and the principal in conferences with parents to address their children's performance. Parents are understandably intimidated and defensive toward a team of educators who point fingers and offer solutions or ultimatums. Occasionally during these meetings, I've been compelled to make referrals to outside agencies for family counseling, rarely with much impact. I rationalize my inability to make these families "right" by saying to myself, "Who am I to dictate to others what conditions they need to raise their kids?" As expected, the parents carefully explain to me that it is their child who is problematic anyway.

Other times at these meetings, the team members identify that children are lacking social skills. Questions about how students get along with others and about how students handle conflicts are asked. Then the other team members look to me for solutions. I feel helpless because my previous attempts to guide students toward healthier interactions have been unsuccessful. Discussions in my office about "I" messages and steps to handle conflicts are ineffective when children get pushed and cajoled into fights. Besides that, many children are motivated by the fame a good fist-fight brings among the entire school community.

Trying to find my way in writing this essay, I identified a recurring situation where I feel most inadequate. I bring my attitude of unconditional acceptance to an environment that is only willing to accept students who eagerly learn like all the other regimented students. All too frequently when I arrive at school, teachers corner me to explain how terribly one of their students is behaving. I can see the disappointment on the teachers' faces when I don't react with shock and amazement that students could actually behave in unproductive ways. I stand there wondering if I should listen to these teachers moan about students whom I find interesting by their approach to achieve uniqueness. By listening, am I helping teachers find an avenue for catharsis, or am I supporting their conviction that I'm going to be able to provide relief by changing students to fit teachers' ideal images?

Teachers want answers from me. I have read everything I could about how to empower children to behave on their own behalf. I have carefully selected materials and handouts about children's behavior so that I can be a resource to these teachers to help make things better. Yet this isn't really what the teachers are asking for. They wish to make a referral to counseling so I can uncover deep-seated anger, relieve it, and send children back to class eager to please the teachers. I pacify teachers by taking these students to my office and connecting with them on a human, personal level knowing it won't meet the teachers' needs. Then I justify this to myself by noting that these frequently are children who are starving for supportive, accepting, encouraging, respectful relationships anyway. My feelings of inadequacy are grounded in the increasing awareness that I can't deliver the changes in children's behavior that the teachers want me to.

With several antecedents listed out, I felt as though I could establish a specific plan with clear steps to gain control over my feelings of inadequacy. Strangely enough, enlightenment hasn't followed. I remember someone once telling me that good judgment comes from those experiences brought on by bad judgment. I'm seeking to become a part of the fraternity of wise people who consistently make confident, appropriate decisions. Since wisdom comes from experience, perhaps the confidence I seek must slowly develop over time.

To find my way, I must promise to examine my feelings and reactions to my experiences. When I feel overwhelmed, I must attempt to figure out why. I must try to figure out who owns the problem I'm being asked to solve. I must delve into my experiences to identify what or whom I'm reminded of from the past. Maybe in 10 years wisdom will have arrived. Then I can write another article to guide new school counselors by telling them how I found my way and how they can find theirs.

CHAPTER 3

WHEN WILL I FEEL LIKE A COUNSELOR?

Wendy Lee Logan

I was in shock! I had achieved a feat that made me the envy of all my fellow graduate students. As I was preparing to begin my practicum, I was hired as a school counselor. "This means you get credit for practicum and internship while getting paid and having a job in the field," my friends said. "Lucky you!" I agreed with them. I was lucky. Then came my first day on the job.

The assistant principal began explaining my responsibilities as the sixth grade school counselor and the testing coordinator for the entire school. Then the principal asked me to meet with him that afternoon about possible groups I should be starting and plans that I had for the remainder of the school year. I glanced down at my noticeably new brief-case filled with the standard purple printed dittos that I had collected throughout graduate school: "How To Start A Developmental Guidance Program," "What To Say And What Not To Say to Your Principal," and a favorite ditto that was simply titled "Help! I'm A School Counselor!" I even had my list of facilitative responses just in case I needed them!

As the assistant principal and the principal continued to talk, it began to dawn on me that I hadn't finished my degree yet. I didn't know nearly enough. Everyone was talking to me as though I was a school counselor. Don't they remember? I wanted to yell at them: "But I'm just a student!"

PANIC STRIKES

My agenda for the first week:

1) Develop and implement a needs assessment for teachers, parents and students.
2) Meet with the teachers to explain my ideas for a developmental guidance program.
3) Develop a form for teacher referrals and student referrals.
4) Write a letter to parents introducing myself.
5) Call my own parents and tell them their daughter got a job.
6) Oh yeah, and meet the students.

Suddenly, I was hit with panic. Had I taken this job under false pretenses? No, I told them I was still in school and they knew I had two semesters left before I graduated. Yes, I had experience working in the mental health field. Yes, the graduate program I am enrolled in is one of the best in the area. Yes, I understood the terminology and could probably write one heck of a term paper on any of the above agenda items. But, the problem was that everyone thought I was the school counselor. It even said so on the door to my office. I drove home nearly in tears and still not feeling nor looking much like a school counselor.

I was a wreck! My husband, who is a marriage and family counselor, came home from work to find me sitting in the middle of our living room with Oreos in hand. He knew there was something wrong. Being the good counselor that he is, he asked me, "Are you O.K.?"

I took a deep breath. "No, I am not O.K. I'm afraid. I'm scared I'll start a group and no one will show up. I'm afraid I'll start a group and someone *will* show up. I'm afraid I won't know what to say to the students the first time I meet with them. I'm afraid I'll forget how to ask an open-ended question. I'm afraid I'll say something stupid at a parent meeting. I'm afraid I've been through two years of graduate school training to be a school counselor only to find two semesters before graduation that I haven't learned a thing!"

My husband surprised me with flowers and sat up with me the night before my second day refuting all my self doubts. My friends told me that they believed in me. My professors reminded me of my scholarly track record and assured me that I was indeed ready. Why, with all this support and encouragement, did I still not feel like a school counselor? I began having conversations with myself on a regular basis. "Now, Wendy, you can be a student *and* a school counselor. What difference will a piece of paper make? You only have two classes left. Do you honestly believe that wisdom will suddenly be bestowed upon you as you shake hands and receive your diploma? No, you know better than that. So, when will I *feel* like a school counselor?" I had no answer.

Slowly, I became acclimated to the school and my responsibilities. I began meeting the students and the teachers and only once did I accidentally walk into the supply closet. I wrote a letter of introduction to parents and began getting phone calls. I started two groups. Teachers did refer students. The students did show up. And I did know what to say. I attended several parent/teacher meetings. I spent late nights on my home computer typing needs assessments and letters to teachers. Self referrals from students came regularly. I began to feel more comfortable in the hallways. I waved to parents and students as I learned to recognize them. And, I eventually learned where all the supply closets were located.

'I AM A SCHOOL COUNSELOR'

The end of the school year was approaching. Even with my own strong self criticism, I knew I had done a good job. Teacher and student referrals were pouring in. My predecessor told me that I had seen more students in the first four months that I had worked there than she had in her first two years. My groups had gone well. I had been observed, evaluated and assessed by my principal, my site supervisor and my practicum supervisor. All reports would indicate that indeed I had performed the role of school counselor well. I felt good. But, I still did not feel like a counselor. I consoled myself. Maybe once I graduated in December . . . Maybe once I worked a full school year . . . Maybe once I reached tenure . . . Maybe when I finally retire . . .

Two weeks before the end of the school year, the other school counselor and I took several sixth graders back to their former elementary schools to talk to the fifth graders about what they could expect in middle school next year. I stood in the back of the room listening to my colleague and three of our students talk to a fifth grade class. The students talked for awhile and the fifth graders asked questions. My colleague explained about the school counseling office and what she does as a school counselor. One of the sixth graders who I had seen for several individual sessions, suddenly interrupted. "And you see Mrs. Logan back there?" He pointed to me as the class turned around to see who would cause such excitement. "She's the one you go to when you really need to talk. That's what I do." And as he smiled, suddenly, I felt it. *I am a school counselor.*

CHAPTER 4

SO LITTLE TO GIVE

Meetu Khosla

As a beginning counselor in India, I often felt frustrated because my education emphasized theoretical knowledge and scholarly inquiry to the exclusion of any practical involvement. The decision to become a counselor emerged from my desire to help the suffering people of India in the most effective, economical, efficient and humane way. Though it was a wonderful opportunity to apply academic knowledge to real life problems, I was a little hesitant because of the emotional challenges I would be experiencing in this field. I wondered if I, a very sensitive person, would be able to handle hearing of the clients' pain and respond in a helpful manner.

I'll never forget the excitement of my first day as a counselor in a hospital where I had the opportunity to work with two clients. Each day, my expectations rose and I would go the hospital with high hopes that more clients would arrive, but after a week, there were no clients. I would sit in my office for hours reading a psychology book. I had two patients in two months with no follow-ups. People began doubting my expertise and I doubted myself because I had so little to offer. In fact, the whole concept of counseling was also under attack by one of the senior doctors. How could I help someone in distress when I wasn't qualified to give medicine? My frustrations got ahead of me and I started feeling depressed. I would go home highly dejected and pour my worries onto my parents.

Finally, I realized that I could no longer depend on my mother's nurturance and my father's guidance to get me through. I had to be brave enough to stand up for myself and my profession in various committee meetings at the hospital. I learned to face the senior doctors who would avoid me because they thought I was a human x-ray machine—fearing that I could read their secret thoughts, feelings and beliefs. Most of the Indians feel this way. "You are a counselor, so tell me what's in my mind," "Tell me my future."

In my country, perhaps like your own, people hesitate to approach a counselor for help due to the stigma attached to it. There are many misconceptions about the nature and use of our profession and it is believed that it is meant only for "crazy people." The senior doctors would always bombard me with never-ending questions: "Is counseling effective?" "Does it help to solve problems?" "Can it reduce the symptoms?" I had to convince them that counseling plays a very important role in acquiring insight into and providing relief from the complexities of our daily lives and improving interpersonal functioning. Gradually, I became accepted and my referrals increased. Yet I still felt that I had so little to give.

As clients would come, I would try my best to be helpful, to patiently listen to their painful experiences with empathy and work out a plan to reduce the gravity of the problem. As the number of clients increased, my self-confidence grew. But I have realized that the path I have chosen is lonely, uneven and stressful. Medical doctors seem to have so much to offer compared to my feeble contributions.

Sometimes clients' problems are clear, but the means of handling them are complicated. Sometimes clients refuse to cooperate and expect immediate relief. Believing that counselors have magical powers that allow them to see through people, they expect miracles. "You know my problem, so tell me what to do." Some parents bring in their troubled children and expect me to cure them in one session. "Talk to him and make him well." These illogical and arrogant demands indicate a lack of awareness about counseling. It also makes me feel even more pressure to be what they expect—a miracle worker.

How can I find my way and help others to do so when I have so little to give? How can I help people when they don't understand what I do?

Dealing with difficult clients is also very frustrating for me. They refuse to open up about their problems, are rude and distrust my intentions. They wonder aloud whether I am really interested in helping or am I merely out to make money. I don't know how to solve this dilemma of the relatives pressuring me to continue treatment and the clients disrespecting me and my profession, shattering my ego into a hundred pieces.

Another hindrance to my success as a counselor is my age. Many times individuals will make appointments but leave after seeing my young face saying that they just remembered some very important work that needs to be done right away. Some have even had the courage to tell me that they expected a much older person. They doubt my ability, saying that I have not experienced life as much as they have so how could I possibly help.

At times there are emergency cases of suicide due to marital, school or work problems. Once a woman called up pleading, "Please come, my 15-year-old daughter is going to commit suicide." I left my annual family function to counsel the girl for two hours. As usual, she didn't come for follow-ups. I often find myself too much concerned about the clients and continue to worry about them even after the client and his or her relatives have moved on. I kept wondering and worrying about this suicidal girl. Finally, after six months, the woman came to the hospital to thank me for saving her daughter's life. I didn't know what to say.

Even though the counseling profession has grown during the past few years, the practice of counseling still lags behind in India. Nobody wants to see a counselor until they find that they don't have any other choice. Even though we can give them what they want—a way to resolve their problems and to obtain relief—sometimes it seems useless. Indian people give a lot of importance to family name, heritage and values and go to great lengths to protect them. They prefer to be self-contained in case of a problem and would rather seek help from a general practitioner or from God, whom they have immense faith in.

Medicine is an immediate solution for organic problems, having life or death implications for the person and counselors cannot escape this reality. But counselors are able to contribute much more to medical care than most doctors and people realize. Apart from physical health and survival, it is important for a person to be emotionally and socially happy. Counselors enable and facilitate psychological growth and development by helping others use their existing resources and skills in a better way and by guiding them in developing new ways to help themselves. Even though we, as counselors, may feel that we have so little to give, it is really much more than we think.

CHAPTER 5

MEMORIES OF BEING A BEGINNING COUNSELOR

Jeffrey A. Kottler

One of the things that makes life so difficult for many beginning counselors is the belief that they are the only ones who feel inept and unprepared to handle the realities of daily practice. When compared to experts in the field, or even to those practitioners with a few years' experience, beginning counselors appear more hesitant, insecure and self-conscious about what they feel they should know and be able to do.

Of course, this is only natural, because without opportunities to test concepts and skills learned in one's training, there is no way to tell how good you are and where you can improve. No matter how good your practicum and internship experiences were, no matter how intensive the supervision you received, there is a different set of expectations and rules for professional counselors than there is for advanced students and interns.

Every professional counselor, regardless of his or her competence or reputation as an expert in the field, was at one time a beginner. Many years ago, the authors of our major theories, the leaders of our professional organizations, the supervisors of our job settings were just as tentative and awkward in their work as today's beginners. I have invited some of the prominent practitioners in the field to share their reflections about their first year on the job. Perhaps their brief stories will provide some degree of comfort to those counselors who wonder whether they will ever find their own way in the profession.

I promised a few of our contributors that before I presented any of their embarrassing anecdotes, I would first present my own—to demonstrate good faith about how lost I felt my first year as a professional. Actually, I would like to tell you about my very first client and how completely unprepared I was to work with him.

I was among the first doctoral counseling students assigned to an internship in a psychiatric facility. At the time, community agency and mental health counseling were brand new specialties. Even though my training was in the areas of developmental assessment, career guidance and individual and group counseling (as opposed to therapy), I found myself among psychiatrists, psychologists and social workers, working with severely disturbed clients.

My very first client was a man whose aroma entered my office before he stepped in—in a stifling blanket of cheap cologne. "Doc," he said, addressing me in a way befitting the white lab coat I was required to wear, "you got to do something about the smell."

Thinking he meant the perfume he had drenched himself in, I waited patiently with my best reflective listening for him to continue. It seemed that the smell that had been bothering him was not of the cologne but of what he was trying to cover up—the smell of cows. He, therefore, asked me in his most earnest voice, leaving no doubt that he was utterly serious, if I would please cut off his nose for him so the cow smell that was haunting him would finally go away.

I looked around the room for help, but there was none to be found. I was truly on my own. Yet, here was this person expecting some help; I had no choice but to continue. The man, you see, liked to have sex with cows. He explained to me without the slightest embarrassment why this was such a great deal for him since he was almost never rejected. To this day, I am amazed that I did not faint or laugh or flee from the room. I just did what I had been drilled so hard and so long to do—to listen compassionately and without judgment, to try to help him understand the meaning of his behavior and what his nose might be trying to tell him. I lived through that first encounter as a professional counselor. I even think that I may have helped him a bit, although I refused to cut off his nose.

Louis Paradise, from the University of New Orleans, remembers a first client: "Being an overly verbal person, and one who probably talks too much anyway, I'll never forget my first client. While it was almost 20 years ago at a small liberal arts college counseling center, it is indelibly etched in my mind. The client was extremely laconic; he barely said a word. There was so much silence that it seemed the interview went on for two or three hours. I was so certain that I had done poorly, I thought I should find another profession. When my supervisors and colleagues heard the recorded tape of the session, they were, quite surprisingly, impressed with my ability to deal with silence. Fortunately, this was in the days before videotape—if they could have seen the way I must have looked, they would have had quite a different impression of how uncomfortable I appeared."

Michael Altekruse, of the University of North Texas, shares another example of the uncertainty he felt when he was just starting out as a school counselor in the same school where he had been a teacher: "My first day on the job began with the home economics teacher bringing me a young man who was known as a 'troublemaker,' 'I want you to fix him,' she said. I took the boy in my office and we both sat down. My new-counselor face must have been pretty transparent because he opened up the conversation with: 'You're in a lot of trouble, aren't you, Mr. Altekruse?' He went on to say, 'It must be difficult to have the school troublemaker thrown at you on the first day of your new job.' I came back with my best counselor response when I asked him what I should do about that. He replied, much to my surprise: 'I had you in class and you were a good teacher and I kinda like you, so just for you, I'll behave in home economics class, but nowhere else.' My fame and expertise spread throughout the school very rapidly.

"Two weeks later, an English teacher came to me with a concern about a boy in her class who was just like the troublemaker I had already 'fixed.' Although I agreed to meet with the child, I felt so overwhelmed with other responsibilities that I forgot to keep the appointment with him. A week later, however, the English teacher also began to sing my praises because she believed I had cured him as well.

"Being very honorable, I felt a need to confess to the English teacher that I had never seen the boy, that her perception of his changed behavior was actually the result of how she was treating him differently. Because my concern for the child was greater than maintaining my own sense of honor, I said nothing to the teacher until the end of the year."

These first three examples of experiences with one's first clients point to how common it is for beginners to feel overwhelmed with all the requirements of their new role and the need to find ways to keep things in perspective.

Peg Carroll, from Fairfield University in Connecticut, remembers how she tried to stay on top of things her first year: "Entering the field of school counseling, an area perpetually filled with fog and grayness as viewed by teacher, student and parent, I devised a vehicle that would provide a concrete way to analyze and examine my everyday activities. I made a chart so I might check each activity as it happened. Each time was specific. For instance, the kind of phone call, the person counseled and the type of interview we had were all noted on my chart. It became routine for me to reach under my blotter and check the necessary category each time I was involved in any activity that was part of my job. At the end of my first year I was able to use these data to make clear decisions about my role as a school counselor. This approach was among the most meaningful acts of my beginning years as a counselor."

This need for new counselors to get a handle on the multitude of new tasks they must face on a daily basis is a common theme among many practitioners, both past and present.

Beverly O'Bryant, Past-President of ACA, reminisces about her first year in the field and about an event that shaped her whole career: "My first experience as a counselor began after returning to school in March after a maternity leave. Upon entering my post, I was encouraged by the principals of my two elementary schools to attend ACA's annual convention. Pleased with the opportunity to enter the profession with such a wonderful beginning, I headed off for five days to convention land. I studied the abstracts every night and plotted each day's activities as if it were a do-or-die mission. I attended as many content sessions as I possibly could and still found time to visit the exhibit areas to order materials from every publisher. I collected handouts from poster sessions and ordered them from sessions that I couldn't attend.

"This convention was one of the most powerful experiences of my professional life. Yet, in spite of how much I learned in the programs, I was most grateful for the counselors I met from all over the country. To this day, some of my closest friends are people that I see every year at the annual convention. I left that convention exhilarated, exhausted and ready to conquer the world."

The reminiscences of these prominent counselors highlight the doubts, the uncertainty and the resolve that are part of being newcomers to the field. Each contributor hoped that by sharing a memory from their first year in the profession, they could comfort others just starting out. At one time, we all have felt overwhelmed by what is expected of us.

We also hoped that experienced practitioners, as well, might be stimulated by these anecdotes so they would revisit their own first years as counselors. Such a journey can help us to recapture the innocence, the zeal, the determination that once helped us to find our own way through professional challenges and personal obstacles to become expert counselors.

PART II

FEELING LOST

CHAPTER 6

CAUGHT IN THE MAZE, AGHAST WITH THIS PHASE

Myrna B. Alexander

Like so many counselors, I too entered the profession seeking closeness with others, the opportunity to learn and grow personally and help people on their journeys. Having been an avid conference attendee, contributor to the field and cultivator of my 22-year-old professional career, I have many colleagues who, over time, became my friends. I would eagerly anticipate seeing these people at meetings, seminars, or simply gather for lunch to chat about our professional involvements and personal lives.

However, during the last several years, I have noticed that I have had to let go of these stimulating and enjoyable encounters with my colleagues to devote more time to the tedious and gruesome, yet necessary, tasks of arguing with insurance companies, entering data into a computer, wading through the bureaucracy of managed care procedures, and playing telephone tag for days or weeks.

As one example of following through on a managed care case, I typically have to dial numerous numbers, speak with different case managers, give repeated clinical reports and make three times the number of phone calls that one would expect to relay such information. In doing this, it is often difficult to maintain my patience, let alone feel any sense of human connection. Usually, there is the proverbial "Press this number if you want this. Press this number if you want that," so that by the time I have completed this impersonal, mechanical procedure, I speak to some distant person who is either uninformed about the particular case or seems naive about clinical dynamics, or worse yet, I get an answering machine! This last option perpetuates the circularity of phone calls devouring my time and spirit.

Then, there are the forms. The opening case forms, the follow-up forms, the consent of information release forms, the closing case forms, the insurance reimbursement forms . . . to name a few. To process the case and receive payment, the "provider" (what a word!) must complete these forms and then fax or mail them to the designated locations. With the fragmentation of services, it is not unheard of for one managed care or employee assistance service to have multiple destinations for the forms, only adding to the complexity, time and effort. For these reasons and many more, a number of excellent clinicians have opted not to join managed health care and employee assistance firms.

As organizations continue to merge, amalgamate, reorganize and downsize, people seem increasingly "caught in the maze," feeling agitated, frightened, skeptical, impatient and irritable. Such emotions are highly contagious and easily absorbed by the counselor involved in case management, not to mention the variations of pain that the counselor is regularly exposed to by the inherent nature of counseling per se. For example, when employees are feeling threatened by impending job loss due to organizational restructuring, their patience is often scarce and their anger can be quick. This, combined with the various nuances of depression, fear, confusion, frustration and irritability ringing in the counselor's ears daily, can create quite a melange of unrest for those of us who work in this field.

I often wonder about the make-up of the counselor amidst this jumble of impersonalism, futility, hi-tech fragmentation, meaninglessness and loneliness. As for myself, I am finding I must reach out more deliberately to my colleagues and friends to restore the lost intimacy and interpersonal connectedness I used to experience quite regularly. I make it a point to call my friends and colleagues to share personally and professionally.

One of my favorite pastimes is to attend conferences. I vary these in clinical subject matter, as well as in format, that is, from the more didactic lecture conferences to the more experiential, residential retreat conferences. This helps me to remain state of the art, interpersonally connected and emotionally and intellectually stimulated.

To counteract the impersonalism of bureaucratic procedures and organizations, I have decided to draw upon my own enthusiasm and warmth to create human networks of nurturance and personalism. I have volunteered my time in holding an official position in a professional organization, giving me many opportunities to network with interesting professionals, as well as extend my support on behalf of the organization. Additionally, I devote considerable time every month to attend professional conferences where I can delight in renewed learning and make human contact. Also, I have accepted a graduate teaching position in counseling which fulfills my desire to provide mentoring and help others grow. Occasionally, I find time to join colleagues for lunch and the interpersonal face-to-face sharing that I find so exhilarating.

There seems to be a crying need for what Carl Whitaker has referred to as "huddle groups," a place where counselors unite in mutual support, peer interaction and supervision. Rather than passively pondering the plight of our profession, in our current age of impersonalism and anomie, I am initiating an active stance of connectedness and human networking. Relaying these experiences to you through this chapter is part of my on-going effort to encourage an open sharing of feelings and invite feedback from others. Who nurses the wounds, feeds the hunger and dries the tears of the counselor "caught in the maze, aghast with this phase" of our professional evolution? Surely, as counselors, we have learned something about healing wounds and taking action! This is one of the greatest challenges facing counselors today and perhaps the creative ways in which we address it may determine the survival of our profession and the well-being of our clientele.

CHAPTER 7

BEING AN "UH-HUH COUNSELOR"

Samuel T. Gladding

My first position as a counselor was in rural North Carolina. I had just finished my master's program. I was so excited about my new position that I graduated in the morning and drove 40 miles to the mental health center that had hired me so I could begin work that afternoon. I didn't even think of going to my apartment nearby until after the center closed. To put it mildly, I was in love with the opportunity to finally function as a professional.

My dreams of what I would encounter and what actually happened, however, were soon to be on opposite sides of a great divide. Before taking the job at the mental health center, I had interned at the counseling center of my university. The students were smart and my natural inclination was to let them work at a speed that was comfortable for them. The word "confrontation" was not in my active vocabulary. Instead, I "reflected," "empathized," and gave "positive regard." Carl Rogers was my hero and I was definitely person-centered. Wonderfully enough, the theory worked and my clients got better. Kidding, I told a fellow classmate that I was the "uh-huh counselor" because I said so little so often.

However, my clients in the rural part of the Tar Heel State were not like the people I had left back on campus. Instead of being generally "smooth and sophisticated," they were often "rough and unrefined." They were not always clean and neat, and their verbal skills were not always good. They were different from me and from most of the people I knew. I was shocked!

"We need better clients," I thought. Yet, none arrived. When I said "uh-huh" nothing happened. When I gave positive regard, empathized and reflected, there was usually little change and often much frustration. I remember after one session, a client innocently asked me: "Have they got any better counselors around here than you?" (I assured him that our sessions would get better.) The question led me to begin reading theory again only days after I thought I had finished reading it forever.

To my delight, when I began discussing theory, I discovered an added dimension about my fellow colleagues. One had trained as a family counselor. Another had a strong background in behaviorism. Still a third was cognitive in her orientation, and the psychiatrist at the center employed a psychoanalytic approach.

I also learned something about myself. Instead of trying to be strictly a Rogerian, I realized that I could be more flexible and skilled. I could become versed in my colleagues' theories and still be person-centered when appropriate. The more my colleagues taught me, the more I was willing to learn from them. It was cyclical. And after all, I didn't want another client asking if there were better counselors around. I knew there were. Reality was tempering my idealism.

From that beginning, I became aware that the first year on the job is as much a learning experience as any graduate school. The process of assimilating information is not measured by tests or role plays but by the successful resolutions that clients come to in regard to their concerns. Just as one size doesn't fit all, being a one-theory clinician does not usually work. In addition, I began to get a real feel for what the word "effective" meant, at least for me.

Before my mental health center experience, I knew mechanically how to go through the motions of saying the right words and taking the proper action. I was somewhat like a child with a bat swinging the same way regardless of where the ball was pitched. In other words, I was not particularly skilled in knowing when and how to respond to clients. To my amazement and delight, I found that I was able to trust myself to a greater extent when I learned more about theory and the experiences of my colleagues. Consequently, I became less fearful of making mistakes, and my clients and I were more in harmony. I learned to trust myself and the counseling "process." I realized that becoming a practitioner takes an artistic touch, as well as a scientific base. Being able to express one's thoughts with a style that resonates with the background of one's clients is an essential skill. It is similar to connecting for a "hit" instead of "striking out."

In this process of growth, I became increasingly aware of my need for further education. I joined the local and state counseling associations. My former professors had already persuaded me to join the national association. By attending professional meetings, I gained support and input outside my work setting. In addition, I found that most pre-senters welcomed questions and comments and were willing to spend extra time with me if I asked them to. Thus, I received some great individual tutorials my first year out.

I kept records of my clients that first year. I began to reread my notes after about six months. To my surprise, some of the adjectives changed. I no longer focused as much on the outer qualities and back-grounds of these individuals. Instead, I concentrated more on their willingness to address the concerns that brought them to counseling. I noticed that I was more attuned to the resources my clients had and the language they used. I was still collaborative and warm personally but I was making a transition as much as any of my clients. I was working with them on their inner strengths and potentials. What I tried to ac-complish with them was in line with their abilities. I was no longer afraid to push them to examine areas they would not have previously explored. What they did was their decision, but I learned to confront in the best sense of that word.

Having now worked in two other states, Connecticut and Alabama, and returned to North Carolina, I occasionally travel to the site where my career began. Each time, I have the special feeling of returning home to a place where I found an identity through reaching out for knowledge, colleagues and growth.

I know that the awkward beginnings are history and in that I re-joice. But I'm thankful for all the memories and what they taught me. When I visit that mental health center now, I seldom say "uh-huh," un-less I am drinking a Pepsi. Instead, I share my thoughts with those I meet and think again of how important it was (and is) to be open to experiences after one's formal education has ended.

CHAPTER 8

LOOKING BEYOND THE TEST SCORES IN CAREER COUNSELING

Vicky Phillips

I ran into a piece of my own psychological past a few days ago: my first Strong-Campbell Interest Inventory, completed a decade and a half ago when I was a junior in college. I remember my two session test-and-tell introduction to career counseling, but the feelings revived by studying my old SCII were not joy. What I felt was a long dormant yet still poignant sense of psychological pain and confusion. My first exposure to counseling had profoundly affected my future career path, though not in a way you may expect.

I spent much of my young adulthood confused. I was a first generation high school graduate who found college academically easy, but socially mysterious. I grew up in a rural Midwestern town where my father was a gas pump jockey and my mother a waitress—neither with high school degrees—but both determined to own their own businesses. The only "college" people I knew before arriving on campus had been my teachers. Accordingly, my career knowledge was Lilliputian, extending no farther than doctor, lawyer or teacher.

After graduating at the top of my high school class, I attended a private liberal arts college on scholarship. This financial aid let me enter a place of social and intellectual privilege, but my mastery of academics aside, my knowledge of the professional career world and my place in it remained meager. Would I ever become a professional? If so, what kind, and how would I start? It did not help that my parents and siblings asked these same questions as I stood before them, Phi Beta Kappa key in hand, promising to open social, economic and professional doors that I could not yet imagine for myself. Or would I?

The first career counselor I turned to for guidance affected my life greatly—even more than I would have liked. Her directive to me was clear: "Whatever you do, *don't* go to graduate or professional school." Confused, I listened to the counselor with both ears, but even more deleteriously with my whole heart. Doctoral study went out the window for me that day. The counselor gave me no reason why I should not go to graduate school. None, except that she was sure I would not be happy with an advanced degree based on my test results.

Why did my first trip to a professional counselor affect me so negatively? First, what the counselor said was not anything that my own harshest inner voice had not already said. I knew nothing of the social or economic meaning of college at that time. It was, for me, a place of intellectual privilege where great ideas would forge more just societies. I was ill-informed by my youth and a decidedly blue-collar vision that did not know—but had wildly imagined for generations—what higher education might be.

Why did the counselor tell me *not* to go on with my education when I had always excelled at education? The back of my SCII score report gives one clue in hindsight. My Academic Orientation (AOR) score was only 38. On the back of my SCII was written: "The AOR scale contains items that discriminate between students who do well in academic settings and those who do not, and as such can be considered an 'Occupational Scale' for 'college students.' Students graduating with a B.A. from a liberal arts college average about 50, M.A.s about 55, Ph.D.s about 60. The item is heavily oriented toward science and the arts (weighted positively) and business and blue-collar activities (weighted negatively)." I was *not* college material, at least in my attitudes. My counselor had simply reiterated what the test had revealed.

What did I hear that day about myself and my future? At the age of 19, already confused, I stood officially advised that I was an impostor. Doors slammed shut that day. I did not find out more about who I might be, but instead was told who I *never* would be. Things were taken from me, not given to me as I had hoped. The cardinal sin of bad counseling was committed upon me on that day. There was no exploration of the deeper meaning of the AOR scale when looked at in light of my love for and excellence in mental work. There was no discussion that my higher scores on "non-academic" items came from my class immersion in these things as a child.

No mitigating factors were discussed. There was no real discussion of what my profile indicated I might be good at or enjoy. My SCII indicated a "very high" interest in business management and the social sciences as well as the aforementioned "blue-collar" themes. I could and should have been told that *combining* business and social sciences might suit me well. That kind of future was strongly indicated, and is what has come to pass.

The bothersome part of this personal professional story? What I received as career counseling 15 years ago is not necessarily much different than what I might get if I were to try again today. I wish I could say I was being cynical about that, but the clients I see and the literature I read inform me otherwise. The two session test-and-tell approach using computer-generated results remains the mainstay of the profession. Career counseling is imagined as the uncomplicated "quick lube" of the counseling profession. What was missing from my career counseling experience 15 years ago, and is still absent in many practices today, was any recognition that career counseling is personal counseling—as personal, vital and complex as is mental health counseling.

Career counseling is not as simple as testing someone, stop watch in hand, to see what kinds of work they seem to have the aptitude or education to do. That might be career assessment, but that is *not* career counseling. Changing or establishing a career is a process that *always* triggers deep mental health issues: family-of-origin positioning, risk-taking, aptitude, self-esteem issues, social status and positioning, and gender identity questions, among others. When one embarks on a career quest there are social and economic landmines all along their way. There are forces within, the psychological, and forces without, the sociological and economic, which must be addressed. The daughter of an illiterate gas pump jockey does not grow up to wear the professional Cinderella suit of a college professor or an entrepreneur who establishes an innovative counseling center. Or does she? In a time of great social mobility and economic flux such questions of hope and change are put to career counselors daily. They are not easily answered.

To the degree career counselors help people define themselves, we also help people delimit themselves. We teach people to let go of certain careers so they may truly take hold of others. We should be very careful, then, when we begin to tell people who they are or might be based on computer-generated reports. We should never forget that career tests are little more than statistical illusions of the "averages" among many competing possibilities. We should never forget that real clients do not consult us in hopes of finding their place on the big mythical bell curve of social science research.

The lesson I learned from my first counselor was an important one: never test-and-tell as if career counseling were an impersonal happening. The results of a computer-generated print-out are *not* as accurate as the ingredients on a label. Learn who the client really is and what his or her world is like.

Sigmund Freud believed there were only two things that could cause neurosis in the modern world: love *and* work. Unfortunately, in separating love or the province of human relationships from work, Freud established a false counseling distinction that still exists today. Mental health counselors are expected to deal with the whole of love or relationship issues. Career counselors are only called in to look at the supposedly superficial issue of adjusting to the work world. Mental health counselors require and demand protracted sessions to deal with "personal" issues, while the career counselor's standard remains the quick two session test-and-tell.

The real key to good-enough career counseling today lies in a decidedly post-Freudian approach. Today's career counselor must perform in the yet unlit arena where love and work increasingly intertwine. In contemporary society, people are offered opportunities to choose from many kinds of work and increasingly believe that they are *entitled* to enjoy if not love their work. Accordingly, if today's career counselor accepts that what she or he does is so simple and concrete that it can be done in two to three hours, then we are selling our profession disastrously short.

CHAPTER 9

STRUGGLING TO SEE
THROUGH THE TEARS

Jeffrey A. Kottler

Despite some twenty years in this field, I still feel puzzled most of the time about what is going on in my counseling sessions, and whether what I think is going on is really what is actually taking place. How can I find my way as a counselor, and help others do so, if I am not altogether certain where we are going? Or, I think I know where we are headed, but I am not often sure whether there might not be somewhere else we should be going instead.

Consider the impact of crying as one example. Like most counselors, I have spent a lifetime in the company of tears. I don't like being around people who are crying (mostly because I think it reflects something I did wrong) but I have accepted that it comes with the professional territory. I have learned, over time, to be around clients who are crying and at least pretend that I am not unduly disturbed by their emotional displays and am able to work with them constructively.

I know that crying is connected to the larger picture of emotional communication. I know that in group and family sessions, in particular, crying is not only inevitable but a desirable sort of interaction that signals intimacy, deep level exploration and intense affective arousal, all desirable goals.

So now I think back to one particular group session that had somehow become very intense, very confusing, very quickly. We join the participants at a crucial moment when intense, complex emotional sparks are flying, all ignited by the tears of one person.

Myrna is speaking through her tears, a veil that is cloaking her contorted face. She describes the years of humiliation she suffered at the hands of a mother who could not love her and a husband who loved her so much she was not permitted to be a separate person. I sat there as the group leader, trying to decide whether to let this develop further or move on to something else. There is definitely some emotional communication taking place but I can't figure out what it means.

Confirming my worst fears, I notice anger simmering, then boiling furiously into rage, etched into the face of another member. Candice can barely hold herself still. Her foot is tapping nervously against the floor, like the tail of an anxious puppy. Her face is set in a grimace, each feature competing for attention as the one most indignant. There is something in Myrna's story that speaks to her.

Fran, however, looks bored, like she has heard this all before. Her eyes flit around the room, looking for a comfortable place to settle. She seems about to speak, shakes her head as if she changed her mind, and continues to scan the room for a place to rest until we have moved on to something more interesting for her. I wonder what it is about Myrna's tears that speak so loudly to Candice but fall on Fran's deaf ears. I feel a headache coming as I try to decode the meaning of all that is taking place.

Two other members, Michael and Floyd, catch each other's attention with their eyes. What is going on with them, I wonder? Have we split along lines of gender? No, apparently not. I see Rachel join them in a smirk. They seem to know something, feel something, that I can't quite grasp.

Then there is me. I am feeling extremely anxious at this point, uncertain where to take us next. I am feeling moved by Myrna's story; a tear forms at the corner of my right eye, deciding whether to hang around for awhile, or let gravity take it for a ride. Yet I am also feeling uneasy. I wonder if there is not some hidden agenda operating. I want to confront Myrna with what I sense is a covert motive, perhaps unintentional, but I have not been all that successful in reading her previously. The language of her tears is one that I can recognize familiar sounds but not quite catch whole phrases.

I look across the group and see Michael watching me carefully. I can tell he senses my unease. In spite of my best efforts to hide what I am feeling, I know, I feel it in my gut, that he reads me like a book. Sure enough, he directs a question my way, but he is really expressing his own doubts about the authenticity of what is transpiring. He is not doing this directly. In fact, he is saying all the right words, the soothing voice trying to reassure Myrna and also strike pre-emptively before Candice explodes. I suspect that I am not the only one who can tell he means something quite different from what he says. We can see it in his body, his face, the furtive eyes and furled lip.

My own anxiety increases. I am clenching my hands, trying to squeeze my heart beat back to normal levels. Emotions are ricocheting across the group so fast I can't catch all the meanings. There is a notable dearth of spoken words, yet the communication taking place is complex, profound and infinitely expressive in its emotional intensity.

What is going on in this group is exactly what happens in our work lives every day. People are attempting to make contact with one another, to be heard and understood, to make sense of what others are expressing. It is often their emotional expression, first ignited by tears, that becomes the focal point of their efforts. And most of the time I feel quite lost, struggling along with them to sort out what is going on and where we should head next.

This particular group session ends on a constructive note. Most of the participants reflect with one another, and in their lives, about the ways they communicate to others they are trying to feel closer to. I do all the right things, all the things I teach to others, about bringing the session to closure. We smile, exchange handshakes or hugs, and rejoin our lives.

I sit alone for a few minutes, trying to make sense of what just took place. If I had to, I could offer several theories to explain what happened and why, what I did, what impact these interventions had, and what participants gained as a result of these efforts. Push me a little further, though, and I will admit to you the extent of my confusion. Do I ever really know what I did that made a difference to any client? Do I ever really understand what it is that I am experiencing at any moment in time? As I sat there in the room alone, musing about how lost I felt, a tear began to trickle down my cheek. Was I moved by what had transpired previously? Was I frustrated by how elusive "truth" is in my work? Was I feeling sorry for myself? Was I exhilarated by the healing power I felt? It was all of these. And none of these.

Isn't it about time that I accepted that being lost some of the time is the price that is paid for traveling life's journey as a counselor? The problem for me is not that I feel bewildered much of the time, in awe of the complexity of what takes place in any session, but that I won't allow myself to live comfortably with this uncertainty, just as I still struggle with my own tears.

CHAPTER 10

USE AND ABUSE OF POWER

Shirley Emerson

"**P**ower is not benign. To do good, one must be willing to do harm."
The speaker was referring to political matters, and I was deep in my
own thoughts, struggling with a problem facing our state licensing board.
A board has power over applicants and licensees. In disciplinary matters, it has power to destroy a counselor's livelihood. The board has the
power to reprimand, to place on probation, to set requirements—such
as further study or supervision—and to revoke a license.

This is not power to be taken lightly. Being a judge was never my
ambition, yet, as president of a state board, that is what I feel like. Sometimes I must decide which party before us is telling the truth, who actually did what and what should be done about unethical behavior.

Where should we focus our concern—on the counselors or their
clients? How does one protect the public and still give the miscreant
some chance to learn and reform? Was the action a single inadvertent
error, or is there a pattern? How do we know? Is the complainer seeking revenge and perhaps stretching the facts, or was a violation actually
committed? One must be willing to make some tough decisions.

Some cases are easy; counselors work with troubled people, some severely so. Sometimes troubled people imagine events that are so prepos-
terous that investigation proves quickly where the trouble lies. These can
be dismissed without harm to anyone. The all-too-frequent charge of inap-
propriate sexual use of a client by a counselor also is easily handled, providing the client is willing to swear under oath. Few think that such a counselor
should be allowed to continue using his or her power over clients who already are in hurt positions when they seek help. Revoking such a license is
as close to a feeling of vindication as one can allow oneself to come.

The term "impaired professional" usually implies abuse of drugs or alcohol, rendering the professional unable to perform with safety, such as a physician dispensing the wrong medication or doing surgery while under the influence. Such impairment in a counselor constitutes grounds for required treatment.

But what of the gray area where there is no substance abuse, no malicious intent, yet—through confusion, impaired judgment and over-zealous involvement with clients—the counselor violates one or more ethical principles?

Such a charge recently came to our board. A colleague was charged with violating ethical principles, involving dual (not sexual) relationships with her clients. The counselor had an excellent reputation and was known as one of the community's very few experts in the area of disso-ciation disorders.

Her clients called in the middle of the night, the middle of dinner and the middle of her life. Her social life revolved around them. She was constantly having an emergency with one or another of them. She even spent vacations calling back daily to talk to whichever client claimed crisis at the time. She expressed fear of people who were "out to get her," to break into her office, to steal her records. Her clients expressed a lot of paranoia. The enmeshment seemed severe.

She was reported to be abandoning one friend after another, and drove one away by accusing her of doing something which the friend did not do. Her behavior seemed to be as dissociated as that which she described in her clients.

At the closed discussion session of the board disciplinary hearing, members agonized over how to treat this case. The evidence proved her "guilt," and she admitted the actions. However, the counselor seemed unable to understand that there was any harm in what she had done, or that she did not always appear in contact with reality. She could not accept that her behavior would have to change.

A licensing board is appointed by the governor to "protect the pub-lic." The public is not protected when a licensee is permitted to violate ethical guidelines, no matter how benevolent or well-intentioned the behavior. To take this person's license would do her harm; it would deprive her of her livelihood. Yet, to allow her to continue her practice would be to allow harm to the public.

The statement from the lecture kept running through my mind: "To do good, one must be willing to do harm." Punishment? Rehabilitation? Harm to the counselor's financial survival or potential further harm to clients? Where is the good one wants to do? Must one do harm?

Board members mandated rehabilitation treatment—therapy, super-vision, restrictions on practice. Since she and I had been close associ-ates in several contexts, I abstained from the discussion and voting, disqualifying myself. Was that the "chicken" solution? Was I protecting my own reputation, her opinion of me? Would the outcome have been different, if I *had* voted? Actually, it might have been more severe, but hindsight is not the point here.

It seems easy, doesn't it? You play, you pay; you sin, you get punished. I hold those beliefs, both professionally and personally. But—why is there always a "but?"—no harm was intended, no sin contemptuously committed. That counselor does not understand that there is a problem. *She just doesn't get it.* She is fighting the therapy, the supervision, all the mandates. Further action may be taken.

Why do I wake up nights wondering? I never thought I feared power. I never thought much about having it. Where does use stop and abuse begin?

Power is a tool, quite necessary to accomplish many changes in society. Now I learn it can be a curse, too. When used to carry out a popular action, it can confer status and popularity. Helping a new trainee through the internship and licensing process to successful professional standing is the easy, rewarding and even fun part of being on a board. When the applicant has done all the appropriate work, the board is barely needed, yet receives all kinds of gratitude. When board members must turn away applicants who are unqualified, or sanction and restrict licensees, however, gratitude is replaced by anger and accusations of abuse of power.

No doubt judges in courts face this daily. I am glad I don't have to—very often. Being both judge and jury is an awesome responsibility.

I could quit. Someone else would be appointed. Someone else would be judge and jury. My life could go smoothly on, the profession would no doubt survive, and I might sleep better.

If one is to be a responsible professional, though, one has to find one's own way. It is the only way. It is a lonely trip. Criticism will come, no matter what the decisions. Perhaps the speaker was correct: One must be willing to do harm if one wants to do good.

Sometimes the harm feels personal.

Sometimes one loses a cherished friend.

CHAPTER 11

HOW TO AVOID
BECOMING A ZOMBIE

Mark E. Young

The counseling profession is hell and it is populated by zombies. That is the conclusion I came to after working in community mental health for five years. I was burned out, or burned up, by a sense of hopelessness after overextending myself to help people and no one seemingly appreciating my efforts. Few clients ever said thank you. Most importantly, they seemed to get better but were never fully self-actualized or cured to my total satisfaction. I thought at this juncture that making popsicle sticks for a living was a good idea. By the end of the day, at least you knew how many you had made.

The hopelessness also comes about because this job is a constant assault on your self-esteem. Something that worked like magic on one client, fails dismally with another. Also, just when you think you know something about getting people better, someone walks into your office with a problem you've never heard of and you are forced into a respectful Rogerian stance, now feeling helpless and hopeless.

The range of clients, and their problems, is astounding. I've had clients who were grieving because their dog was dead, had run over their grandchild with a car, had shot and killed their husband and had been locked in a closet daily as a child and had bulimia, panic disorder and major depression simultaneously.

I've also had clients who had been in therapy longer than I had, who never listened to what I said, who never said more than 10 words in 10 sessions, who actually could not be silent for five seconds and who came once every six months to let off steam and returned with the identical problems.

In case you haven't seen enough horror movies, zombies are both living and dead. They lose their ability to care for others and themselves. They can't even see themselves in a mirror. You can imagine that their job performance suffers as they stumble down hallways with hands outstretched until 5:00 p.m. I entered the shadow realm because I cared about other people and mistakenly believed that I was superior to them and destined to help them. I overspent my bank account of energy, squandered my time on those who wanted it the least and ended up resenting the very people I was trying to help.

I escaped from this twilight existence, but before I talk about that, I want to relate the story of my downfall and how I became one of the living dead. There are five experiences that were instrumental in turning me into a zombie.

EXPERIENCE 1

I went to case conferences expecting supervision and help. A case conference, you find out, is a place you go and discuss a problem client and everybody tries to make you feel better by pointing out what a resistant jerk your client is and what a long-suffering and insightful counselor you are. Another thing that happens regularly is that a few counselors in the agency are willing to express their feelings of inadequacy and hopelessness about their cases and some of the other counselors never seem to present a problem case.

EXPERIENCE 2

I believed in the *Diagnostic and Statistical Manual*. The *DSM-IV* is like Jaws IV, relentless and they keep making sequels. If you believe that thing, your clients are all pretty sick and it'll be a miracle if any of them ever get better. Figuring out someone's diagnosis is fun until you realize that it doesn't get you any closer to helping them. You still have to do the actual counseling. I felt discouraged every time I saw those labels and wondered what miracle would have to occur to cure a major depression.

EXPERIENCE 3

I was overwhelmed with paper work. At one mental health clinic, it took 21 pages of paper work to get someone into the system. I spent the first session questioning them like a detective under hot lights and suggesting that they hold their tears until next session. Paper work, when it made no sense, became a real handicap in the therapeutic process and added to my sense of despair.

EXPERIENCE 4

I blamed my clients and became more confrontational in order to feel like I was doing something. I beat up on a few people to ease my sense of impotency and this ended up making me feel worse. They probably felt worse too. I remember telling a client that he was boring. I am sure I hurt his feelings without really helping him. But I was desperate to make something happen. When my biggest weapons seemed to have little effect, I was convinced that I was a fraud.

EXPERIENCE 5

I searched for the perfect therapeutic system. At various times I was a true believer in gestalt therapy, transactional analysis, bioenergetics, rational emotive therapy, client centered therapy and psychodrama. There were a number of problems with my belief in the Holy Grail of counseling, chief among them being the fact that one system does not fit all.

REJOINING THE LIVING

Now, according to the rules in horror movies, various creatures can be transformed back to their good side with some item you can usually find in your own kitchen. In my search to stay among the living, I discovered a few things that helped keep me from losing heart, or getting a stake in it.

First, I had a supervisor who saved my life. He had a love and fascination for counseling and he took me under his wing when I knew nothing. He let me sit in with him during sessions and we co-led a group for two years. Our long discussions about the nature of counseling, healthy relationships and the role of the counselor were important. But more crucial was knowing that I had someone to consult with when I had a tough client and with whom I was not afraid to show my feelings of ineffectiveness. He always said I was his worst supervisee because I could never be wrong. I was so defensive about my work, I couldn't hear criticism, but he helped me get over that.

Second, I developed a healthy eclecticism. I learned to utilize the techniques from a variety of systems in the service of my client's goals. I started looking to the uniqueness of the client. Only those techniques that meet the needs and values of the client will work. From this, I began to appreciate that clients don't even have to change if they don't want to. That was a big relief.

Third, I continued to do the best counseling I could do with each client until I had some successes. This may sound exaggerated and possibly disappointing to newcomers, but it was not until my seventh year in practice that I felt like I was earning my pay. It seemed to happen suddenly but was really the result of a long development. I was seeing a sixteen-year-old boy who had been diagnosed obsessive compulsive and whose parents were over-involved in his life. Instead of taking a wait-and-see attitude, I dove in and became very active in family counseling. Although I had never felt comfortable with family counseling, there was immediate relief for the client and his parents. I was so surprised that I began seeing the teenager by himself until the obsessive rituals disappeared. Although I became a celebrity to the family, the most important thing that happened was feeling my power to promote change.

That success led to other successes, as well as a quantum leap in my confidence. But rather than making me feel that I could help the whole world, I began to suspect that the therapeutic magic is a subtle thing. I can't make it work on everyone.

The thing that saved me from zombiehood was the realization that I don't have total control over when the magic works. Now, if it doesn't work, I don't blame myself or the client. I find another way. I try something different, I refer, I do something that makes me interested in the client. When I am having a good time in therapy, the client seems to have a good experience.

Now I don't worry so much whether I can help every client. I know that sometimes I will and that joy sustains me in the droughts. There is a sixteen-year-old boy, a nine-year-old girl and a few marriages that remind me that, once in a while, I am a great counselor. That's enough.

PART III

Confronting
Ourselves

CHAPTER 12

FACING MY OWN ISSUES

Marie M. Schrader

It has been two and a half years since I made a decision that changed the direction of my career. I still think about the situation I found myself in—my feelings about it and how I handled things. The truth is I did not handle things at all.

I was working in a university counseling center with a full schedule of counseling and teaching students, sitting on numerous committees, and supervising graduate interns. It was the kind of job that I had dreamed about when I was a graduate student. However, over 15 years of working as an employee at either a college, university, or community mental health agency, I thought about entering private practice. The birth of my second child essentially forced me to make this career decision much sooner than I probably would have. I had wanted to be in control of my work life, in control of my work hours, and have more time to be with and enjoy my children. Who doesn't!

With a new baby, my longing intensified. The pressure to make some kind of change was unbearable. My work structure no longer fit my life. My priorities had changed. I was miserable and depressed in a work life that didn't allow much time with my new baby. For months I felt stuck. However, in this gloomy haze, I realized I did have choices. I made the decision to resign and made plans to pursue private practice. I felt relieved and empowered. My husband was helpful and full of support, although he was concerned about the financial strain.

I felt ready to move on into a new phase of my life. I would create my work structure and work hours. I would raise my children the way I wanted to. I had had enough of society's not so subtle message of career first, family second.

I felt ready. But not as ready as I thought. I was not prepared for the response from my two women colleagues. The three of us were responsible for all the counseling and supervision in the center. Our job title of "counseling psychologist" was one of pride and hard earned credentials. We were compatible and liked working together. There were differences though. I was the oldest of the three and had worked in the counseling field with more years of experience. We had similar educational backgrounds. One colleague was a brand new graduate and this was her first professional position; the other had her degree for some time and was an experienced professional.

When I told them of my decision to resign for the main reason of spending more time with my new baby daughter, I sensed many doors closing from them. I felt a coldness coming over our relationship; they were shutting me out. No more visiting in my office, no friendly office "chats," no more laughter, and good-bye to the feelings of camaraderie. The three of us had shared many lunches and had even spent an evening at my home for dinner. In their eyes, I had become a persona non grata. I was leaving the counseling center for all the wrong reasons. It was not for a better position or promotion, but to stay home with my baby. We were dedicated to counseling women students, in particular, to make life choices other than marriage and family. Here I was, leaving to stay home with a baby and try to develop a part-time counseling practice. It was as if I had betrayed them both. So much for the women's movement, I remember thinking cynically.

We have choices in life, unlike past generations of women, but only if you choose in a certain way, only if those choices move you away from a close marriage and raising children. I had spent my entire life up to this time preparing for and establishing a lifelong career with non-stop undergraduate and graduate education followed by work. I completed my Ph.D. degree at age 25. I was ready to know another way to live—one filled with children. That was, for some, heresy and betrayal. The three of us shared a sense of identity when we began working together, and perhaps my wanting out was confusing to them. We three had felt smug about ourselves. But when I was with my children, I didn't need to feel smug anymore.

In finding my way through this coldness and abrupt withdrawal of friendship, what did I do? I did nothing. They avoided me and I went along with it. I avoided them. They barely spoke to me directly and I barely spoke to them at all. I avoided them at every opportunity. I played at avoidance to perfection. This game dragged on for four months.

I've often rationalized in true RET fashion that it didn't matter what they thought about my decision. I didn't need their permission to change my life . . . I knew what I was doing. I felt confident in my decision to leave and for the very reasons I was leaving.

The truth is, however, their responses and reactions hurt me very much and no amount of rationalizing can change that. I still tried to keep it all in perspective. Intellectually, I was fine, but inside I was really hurting. How many times do I tell my clients to face the emotional issues in their lives? How often do I tell them to confront rather than avoid? Yet there I was avoiding my two colleagues. I felt shut out and I never said a word to them about it. Even to this day. I did not say good-bye to them my last day at work. All the laughter and friendship we shared—everything felt destroyed. And it still bothers me to this day.

The irony in this is I see myself as a behavioral, short-term, brief counseling expert. I see myself as a problem-solving, assertive, directive, and focused counselor. I like to think I can zero in on issues and problems and then spot the problem quickly. But in my emotional life there are discrepancies. I avoided rather than confronted. I sensed confusion and hostility and ran from it. I did not walk away from this conflict, I ran. I'm sure my two colleagues have their own issues with my reasons for leaving but I'm still responsible for my way of responding to them.

In finding my way as a professional, I continue to learn what it means to live what I teach to others. I am finally learning that to be emotionally honest with my clients and students is not enough; emotional honesty must be a part of all my important relationships. My never-ending goals remain to lessen the distance between how I feel and what I teach and counsel. I try to bridge the gap between helping clients confront their issues and avoiding my own. My goals are simple but so difficult—to help my clients deal with their issues and for me to confront my own.

CHAPTER 13

ON BECOMING A
WOUNDED HEALER

Mark Schorr

I was feeling confident, satisfied, after a productive session with a long time client. Minor irritants like paperwork and productivity demands were the only small clouds on the horizon. The message from my wife read, "Bad news. Please call."

It was worse than bad news. During a routine annual checkup, the doctor had discovered my wife had leukemia.

Of course the diagnosis was a mistake, we insisted. Another blood test confirmed the worst. Referral to a hematologist/oncologist. More confirmation. Chronic myelogenous leukemia. The world suddenly was painted gray, tinged with black.

I won't presume to talk about my wife's feelings. Like myself, a perennial worrier, she is handling this with a dignity and courage that I can only admire.

In the past, I thought I understood my clients' depression. Being plunged into a full-blown neurovegetative depression—a 25 on the Beck Depression Inventory—has given me a new understanding of the word.

Nights and mornings were the worst. Four hours of uninterrupted sleep was a gift. Waking, there was the hope that the diagnosis had been part of a bad dream. Then the slap-in-the-face realization that it was real.

I had used the pen name Ann Hedonia on humorous missives. Now I knew her intimately. Pleasure was impossible, occasional distraction was the best I could hope for. We rented movies, but reminders were everywhere. Even a movie like "Quiz Show," seemingly safe, contained references to Geritol (the sponsor) and iron poor blood.

Taking the kids to the park, I could usually romp with them. Now I stood and watched, trying vainly to smile as they showed off their stunts. How much did our five-year-old daughter know? Did she always talk so much about death and disease? Could our two-year-old son sense my anguish?

Thinking about our young children was a personal agony. My wife had quit her job as a nurse to enjoy full-time parenting. We've been married 22 years and envisioned the kids having the luxury of a two-parent home, with a full-time homemaker. An idealized Cleaver family childhood. Full of innocence, occasional mundane concerns. Now this ticking bomb had been tossed into our lives.

Concentrating on anything was difficult. I would reread the simplest paragraphs repeatedly, trying to cut through the depressive ruminating. How could I cope, feeling helpless and hopeless, wanting to be strong but feeling like crying and curling up into a fetal position? What was going to happen? How could the family survive without her?

Normally a voracious reader, I struggled to make it through the morning newspaper. But every bit of sorrow seemed even more sorrowful. During a previous career, as a reporter, I had seen random tragedy strike unsuspecting and innocent people. Of course that would never happen to me, or anyone close to me. The core delusion of existential safety dissolved.

I looked for omens. Finding five dollars, good luck. Hearing a sad song on the radio, bad luck. A rainbow after a storm, proof positive that it would be okay.

I sought to gain control of the situation by gathering data. But even with information that was 75 percent optimistic, the pessimistic 25 percent would haunt me. Still, sleepless nights I cruised the Internet reading sci.med.diseases.cancer, Cancer-L, the Hem-Onc listserv, and Bone Marrow Transplant-talk. Looking for answers, knowledge, a feeling of control. Trying to make meaning out of meaningless misery.

The first weeks were the worst, as the doctor ran tests and we waited for news. Once treatment began, there was a surge of optimism. We were doing something. And when my wife responded to the medication we felt renewed. But the oppressive menace lingered like a monster in the basement. It came upstairs when the first medication failed.

We met with a cancer counselor who balanced helpful information with caring and concern. She provided information not only about the illness, but doctors' personalities, financial concerns, differences we could expect between us, and how to talk to the kids. Seeing someone so empathic made me proud to be a counselor. My wife, initially reluctant to participate, left our sessions feeling recharged.

Friends and co-workers—the two are not mutually exclusive—were wonderful and supportive. We heard numerous stories of survivors of life-threatening illnesses. People volunteered their time to take care of the kids. Others went to the Red Cross to be tested to see if they would be suitable bone marrow donors.

A sense of humor returned. My wife and I were able to joke about our weight loss, and discussed plans to market the Neurovegetative Diet. To look marvelous, all you need to do is feel terrible. In the chemotherapy room there was a copy of a tabloid with an article on brassieres causing breast cancer. We hoped that wasn't the only journal our doctor relied on. We found a copy of a Marlboro products catalog in the oncologist's waiting room, and joked about it being a way to drum up business.

I began seeing a counselor myself. It took me close to two months to finally make an appointment. Why so much resistance from someone who knows what good counseling can do? Was it because I "know it all"? Was it because I didn't want to be the one not taking notes in session? Was it because I was afraid that if it didn't help me feel better, there was no hope? Was it because of the cost? Probably some combination of the four plus the logistics of working the time into an already overloaded schedule. Now, a few sessions into it, I have not experienced a miracle cure. But it feels beneficial to have a place to vent.

In my sessions with clients, there would be frequent reminders of our black cloud. One man complained about a woman he knew—she was weird but that was because she had cancer. Another client had a son who killed himself after he was diagnosed with leukemia. Another came in numb with grief over the recent cancer death of a housemate. When clients would tell stories in which the mention of disease was a minor note, I had to restrain myself from asking questions merely to satisfy my own insecurity. Or to let my mind drift off into worrisome tangents.

Getting into that trance-like state where I am able to really hear people, observe them, focus and empathize, allowed me to set aside my own worries for 50 minutes.

Ultimately, there was the hope that the good that I do in my office will be paid back in some cosmic way. Never religious, I found the old axiom about no atheists in foxholes to be true. In the dead of night, lying in bed staring at the ceiling, I found that prayer was a helpful way to focus my thoughts. I didn't know if I was doing it right, but if football players can pray for a touchdown, I presume that sending out thoughts of healing, in whatever format, should be acceptable.

We wait now for a suitable donor. We visit the oncologist. We schedule a trip to the internationally known center for bone marrow transplants in Seattle. My wife's chemotherapy has the disease under control for now.

Progress is being made every day—in today's paper there's an article about using a baboon's bone marrow to help an AIDS patient—but the procedure itself is more debilitating than heart surgery. Our neighbor was out mowing the lawn one week after his bypass operation—my wife will be recovering for more than six months after the transplant.

The next time a depressed client comes in unable to eat, I won't lecture him on the brain's need for glucose. I know what it is like to hold tasteless food in your dry mouth, with jaws unwilling to work, throat unable to swallow. I know what it is like to feel like you are going crazy because you can't control your thoughts. I know what it is like to think that death is better than the mental pain.

In the long run, this experience will make me a better counselor. Every pothole in the journey does, unless I fall into it. I've learned things about myself, about my relationships, about life in general, that no book or training could offer. Would I recommend this experiential education to anyone? Hell no! But no one really asks for the challenges they face.

We hope that our whole family comes out the other side with a renewed appreciation of life, a renewed commitment to living. And maybe I can give back something to humanity with the wisdom that comes out of pain.

CHAPTER 14

RECOGNIZING YOUR EMOTIONAL VULNERABILITIES

Shan Pincus

Pam was my first client as a professional counselor. I looked forward to meeting her with such unbridled anticipation that I didn't even notice that the air conditioner was broken and the temperature had climbed into the 90s. I fantasized about sitting quietly and listening to Pam with great understanding and much compassion. I just couldn't wait to hear her story.

Pam was already in my office when I arrived. As I stepped through the door she frowned at me, shaking her head. "Excuse me," she said, "nothing against you, but I'm not talking to anyone but Florence." Florence was her previous counselor who had left our clinic for another job.

I was stunned by Pam's rejection of me. Although I attempted to squelch my feelings, it did not work. I was lost. But after wallowing in my disappointment for a few minutes, I tried to see the meeting from Pam's perspective. I wondered what would it be like to speak to a total stranger and soon I began to understand how she felt. Someone whom she had confided in was taken away, and now she was expected to form a new bond. I wondered what I could say that might help Pam trust me. "Should I help you get Florence back?" I asked, believing that this intervention would endear me to her.

"Why did they give me you?" she asked, looking for a tissue to mop her forehead. Again, I felt a surge of frustration envelop me. We were not making contact and I was even beginning to dislike her.

One thing I knew for sure: you can't make it in this profession if you can't keep your clients. I also knew you can't help anyone when your own feelings get in the way. I was afraid Pam might pick up my negative feelings and not come back.

Again, I struggled with my feelings. "You were given to me," I said, in the calmest voice I could muster, "because I knew I could help you." I felt she wasn't buying it. Pam again returned to her repetitive theme. "They're always changing counselors on me," she persisted.

"How do you feel every time you get a counselor changed on you?" I asked. I hoped to get her to vent some of her feelings: anger, sadness, abandonment, longing, grief, anxiety—anything!

Evidently, she had difficulty verbalizing her thoughts and feelings. She shook her head back and forth. "I don't know . . . you . . . I'm not sure."

We sat quietly as I looked at her, waiting for her to make sense of her feelings. I, too, had to come to terms with my own feelings. I was ill-prepared to deal with the assault of my emotions. Despite the pain, I almost wanted to thank Pam for creating this experience for me. If I was going to grow in this field, to find my own way, I had to learn to recognize my interfering feelings and deal with them.

The silence felt more oppressive than the weather. I began to feel anxious, almost faint. Normally, I enjoy the heat and I couldn't believe how it was affecting me. Just as I was wondering why I was having these weird sensations, Pam interrupted my thoughts. "My doctor doesn't want me to be in hot places. He says I could faint because my blood pressure is so high." So that's it—emotional contagion. I had picked up Pam's anxiety. Once I could label what I believed was going on, I was able to relax more. I brought Pam a cup of ice water and assured her she would be just fine. After taking a drink, she too seemed to relax and went right back to her favorite subject, Florence. Although I wanted to hear the story of Pam's life, by now I had no problem listening to how Florence helped her sort out her life, get her GED and find a job. I felt encouraged. My relationship with Pam began to grow. She was speaking to me, even though she was singing the praises of another counselor, and I no longer felt devaluated or rejected.

I continued to see Pam for a while, though somewhat sporadically. Many of our sessions focused on Pam's mother. She told me how her mother gave her to foster care when she was very little because her new stepfather was so abusive. I could see the anguish in Pam's face as she talked about her foster home. Often I wanted to take her in my arms to comfort her. "No one should have had to go through your kind of torment," I said.

"You know," she said, "I like you better than Florence."

"Why is that?" I asked.

"Because you seem to understand me better than she did."

I wanted to hug her.

From my experience with Pam, I learned that counselors will encounter all sorts of emotions while working with their clients. Some feelings that affect us belong to the client. Some feelings simply belong to us. It was essential that I separated my emotions from Pam's. I needed to know what she needed so I could tune my interventions to move her toward emotional growth. At the same time, I also needed to know my own needs in order to sharpen my counseling skills. In that respect, my time with Pam was extremely beneficial to me.

I learned about my own emotional vulnerabilities, perceived feelings of rejection and devaluation. I learned what frustrated me and what made me angry. As I worked though some of these issues, I came to be less emotionally encumbered and more sensitive to my clients. The joy I knew as Pam resolved some of her issues and began to feel more positive about herself and toward me is one of the rewards of this profession.

CHAPTER 15

LEARNING COMES IN MANY FORMS

Holly Forester-Miller

As I look back on my counselor education, two significant events stand out in my mind. They probably influenced my development as a counselor more than anything else in all those years of training.

The first experience occurred when I was a master's degree student taking my laboratory practicum class. I was counseling a 12-year-old boy named Brian. In our first session, as I was practicing empathy to the hilt, Brian started to cry. Instantly, my heart and mind started racing, and I thought, "Aha! It works! I hit on something." Then, "Oh no! Now what? The poor kid. He looks like he is in so much pain. He must be so uncomfortable and embarrassed. It hurts me to see him in so much pain. How can I make him comfortable? Oh, look at those huge brown eyes; he looks like Bambi did when he found out his mother had died."

Well, I quickly changed the subject. Brian obliged and changed gears with me, drying his tears. Although he brought up the original subject twice more in the session, I managed to side-step it and keep the session on a superficial, cognitive level. In other words, I ran like hell. I knew immediately what I *should* have done, but tears from a 12-year-old boy caught me off guard and elicited some of my own scary feelings. So, I played it safe. But—what price did Brian pay for *my* discomfort?

My supervisor helped me to understand my own fears and sort out the issues for me regarding Brian's tears. Maxims such as, "boys aren't supposed to cry," and "I am supposed to help him, not hurt him," rang in my ears. But my next session with Brian was different. He brought up the same subject again, and I did some appropriate empathic responding. Once again, he began to cry. Not only did I let him cry this time; I gave him permission to let go. After he cried for awhile, he went on to tell me that I was the first person who ever allowed him to talk about this subject so freely. I am thankful to Brian—he gave me a second chance to "let him talk."

I learned, then, the importance of being *with* clients, of following *their* leads, and most important, allowing them to express themselves. I made a commitment to learn to be comfortable with my clients' emotions, as well as their thoughts. It took a long time, though, for me to become reasonably comfortable with the intensity of emotional expression. Now when I do a counseling demonstration in one of my classes, and my students say things like "You probably come by this naturally," I tell them about Brian.

Several years later, I had the opportunity to *feel* the importance of being allowed to deal with emotions in counseling. I learned from a personal experience what Brian probably felt in his first session. I was a doctoral student and had gone to the college counseling center to discuss some major life decisions I was facing and to explore an ongoing internal struggle. On the verge of quitting my studies, I poured my heart out regarding my decision between wanting to have a profession and wanting to be a mom. I wasn't sure I could do either of these tasks well, much less both. I then touched on some of the other issues and struggles I thought I might like to work on in counseling.

Amazingly, the very "cognitive" counselor I was talking to managed to solve my dilemma for me in a record-breaking 45 minutes. Imagine. I had been thinking through this issue for months and hadn't resolved it. At the end of the session, he sent me on my way with a solution in hand and didn't even offer me an opportunity for a return visit. I left the office feeling unheard, unimportant and angry. Unlike Brian, I knew what counseling was supposed to be, and this wasn't it. I knew that the client was supposed to be more important than the counselor's ego and feelings. I wondered how it was that this counselor, who had a Ph.D. and 20 years of experience, had not learned that yet.

This experience reinforced what Brian had taught me several years earlier: Acknowledging people's feelings and helping them to express them is a crucial component of counseling (although not always easy for the counselor). It may not be the only therapeutic ingredient, but it is the glue that holds everything else together.

There are lots of potential messages in these two stories. The main one is to open yourself up to all the forms of learning that are out there for you. Do the tough stuff. Don't let your fears and insecurities get in the way of dealing with your weak areas. Take risks. Try the techniques that challenge you, especially while you have a supervisor to help you through it. Be open to dealing with your issues and—most important—experience counseling yourself.

If you wait until your fears go away, you will probably never do things. As a good friend of mine says, "Just hold on to your courage stick and dive in, dragging your fears behind you." As Brian and I can tell you from experience, growth isn't always comfortable. Be willing to allow for your own, and your clients', discomfort.

Chapter 16

From My Heart

Laurie Carty

Finding my way has been a long, lonely and painful journey.

My search, like many others in the helping professions, began early in life. Often, the first lessons of helping begin in the family of origin. As the first born in a family of six children, I assumed the role of caretaker. Our home was full of denial and anger, at times abusive and toxic. I thought it was my job to care for my parents, who often lost control and became violent. I also assumed responsibility for my four younger brothers and my sister. In this home, there was little room for the feelings of the heart.

Growing up in this environment left me with a lifelong legacy of unresolved core issues. I have continued to struggle, both personally and professionally, with themes of loneliness and isolation, anger and pain, power and powerlessness, dependency and the need for approval, lies and truth, and the consuming demons of a recurrent depression. These demons continue to haunt me, at times even threatening my survival.

I escaped my first home when I married; that is, I ran from one prison to another. Consistent with all we know about dysfunctional family systems, I chose a man who would provide me with the same type of emotionally toxic environment that I experienced as a child. In my second home, there once again was little room for feelings of the heart. I remained in this abusive marriage for more than 20 years before I took a sabbatical year to find what was in my heart.

As a nurse, counselor, supervisor and professor in male-dominated academic and hospital environments, I am used to being respected for what is in my head, not my heart. I am used to making decisions from my head, rather than my heart.

In spite of this pattern, I have always believed that the wisdom of the heart must be brought together with that of the head. My problem has been that, even though I trust the hearts of others, I have never been able to trust my own. The way of the heart is not easy. It hurts. It makes us vulnerable.

As counselors, if we are not open to the pain in our own hearts, we are not open to caring and connection with others. A client trapped behind a wall of pain needs to feel cared for and understood. Counselors reach out to clients from the sources of pain locked within their own hearts. It is this process that transcends the isolation of pain and makes it bearable. This experience of caring and connection with the counselor empowers clients to experience themselves as valuable and worthwhile individuals and infuses them with hope.

The road that I traveled has not been a straight one, as is so often the case for those of us trying to find our way. Many experiences and relationships have affected me. One such experience occurred when I was a student during my rotation at a large psychiatric institution. I cannot find the words to describe my horror as I observed the destructive effects of depersonalizing human beings. Many psychotic patients, having given up social conventions to live an existence of hypervigilance, are able to read social interactions with remarkable accuracy, and yet they are often treated as if there was no *person* inside them.

It hurt me when they were herded into the cafeteria for meals. It horrified me when they were lined up, waiting for electroconvulsive therapy. As a student learning to care for clients, I had a great deal of difficulty integrating what my heart was screaming with what my head was telling me. My head was saying, "Get a grip! You are really losing it this time."

I looked around at the other helping professionals. There was no emotion. There was no heart.

I looked at the clients. They were all without emotion. I felt crazy. I remember thinking I would prefer death to the treatment I was observing. I promised I would always keep my heart alive when working with clients. This has not been an easy task.

It has been my relationships with my students and clients that have kept my heart alive. Helping them find a voice for their hearts has allowed me to remain connected with my own. I have worked as a group counselor in a community youth program for many years. I lead groups of young adults, ages 19 to 30, and supervise counseling students leading groups of young people ages 14 to 18. Working in this safe environment, I learned to trust my heart.

As I taught young people the lessons of growth and survival, they taught me the power of the heart. In the safety of a group culture that accepted and trusted feelings, it was possible to take risks and be vulnerable. The expression of feeling was communicated in many forms: through music, art, psychodrama and any other creative medium a group member wanted to try. In this culture, I could express my own feelings.

In the last few years, I have felt increasingly bombarded by stories of abusive relationships. Working with young people who have been abused and who continue to seek abusive relationships has made me increasingly uncomfortable with my own personal relationships. As I struggled to empower students and clients to value themselves and take charge of their lives, I began to feel more and more like a hypocrite.

I tried to deny the effect my personal life was having on me professionally. I attempted to compartmentalize my life. I was a very competent person at work, while at home I vacillated between trying to please and acting out in a dysfunctional dance with my husband. I felt I was two very different people. I told myself it wasn't necessary to disclose the details of my life; it was enough to share my feelings.

I began to find that the indirect expression of my feelings through music and metaphor was no longer enough. I was becoming increasingly aware that the way in which others perceived me and the life I was living were worlds apart. As group members exposed their painful stories of abuse, they believed that I had it all together. Selective self-silencing was choking me. I counseled clients to make the changes necessary to free themselves from a legacy of abuse, but I was asking clients to take risks I could not take.

Because truth, both self-honesty and honesty with others, has always been important to me, these emerging insights about my secret demons could no longer be kept silent. I could not resolve my mounting turmoil, so I decided it was time to follow the advice I had been giving others for so many years: Get some help!

I began my counseling journey with great trepidation. I know this is not unusual: Many of us make the absolute worst clients when it is time to switch roles. We have our control issues and our unwillingness to get out of our heads and into our hearts. I worked very hard to be a good client. I have begun to hear more clearly what my heart tells me. I have even started the process of trusting my heart, even when all the facts are not in place. I am searching for a more direct voice for my heart.

Writing this article is part of my process of bringing my heart together with my head. It is not about blame. Blaming others is a self-defeating behavior that disempowers. Each person who has touched my life also has a story of hurt and pain. Each of us has a choice about what to do with the pain in our lives. The pain can be denied, turned inward to punish the self or externalized to hurt others but the energy from this pain also can be used constructively. My advice for beginners finding their way is to embrace your pain and use its energy to create. Always trust your heart and be guided by your head.

CHAPTER 17

SYSTEMIC DYSFUNCTION AMONG COUNSELORS

Jeffrey A. Kottler

How are we ever to find our way when we spend so much time bickering among ourselves? Be honest. Of all the time you spend in meetings—staff conferences, committees, and all the various gatherings that are organized throughout a typical week—how much energy and effort is actually expended accomplishing anything meaningful?

We argue with one another about who is right (us) and who is wrong (them). We fight for our personal agendas and feel misunderstood and abused when we don't get our way. We listen to colleagues drone on and on about things that hardly matter. We engage in turf wars over issues that have little to do with helping anyone.

A visiting professor from another country once remarked to me in a voice so soft and casual I am not certain to this day whether I heard him right: "How does this help your students?" He had been sitting in on our staff meetings and could not help but notice we spend so much time talking about things that matter so little to so few. "What difference does it make", he wondered, "whether you follow either one of these options? Is that somehow going to make a difference to your students?" Ever since that day I have been haunted by that question and I have measured each issue by the standard of how whatever action we take helps or hinders the quality of student/client services.

Yet it all seems so futile. There are those who seem to thrive on conflict. They genuinely enjoy upheaval and controversy; they like getting in other people's faces, throwing their weight around, proving their potency and sabotaging what others want. In a perfect world, supervisors, administrators and colleagues would exist only to help make our jobs easier. They would support us. They would offer guidance constructively and compassionately.

The reality of counselor practice, however, is that we are our own worst enemies. If we apply systemic thinking to the "families" with whom we work, there is compelling evidence of major dysfunction. Our clients are often triangulated in the battles that we are fighting against one another. If we are demoralized, or worse yet, still reeling from the latest blows of indignity or disrespect from those we work with, how are we to serve others with a clear head and pure heart?

I wonder if our first responsibility is not to the clients and students for whom we exist to serve, but to one another. For every disillusioned counselor, there are dozens, even hundreds of casualties that result from this indifference. For every professor or supervisor who is wounded, these consequences may be several times more powerful. The effects trickle downward.

For example, I perceive that a colleague tries to hurt me, or at the very least, undermine my efforts to carry forth my helping agenda. For reasons known only to him, perhaps because of basic value differences in ways we operate, I suffer mightily. As hard as I try, I can't let my feelings go. I feel discouraged this day, even beaten down. In my wildest dreams can I possibly imagine that I will be optimistically helpful to my clients, students and supervisees in the next few days? Try as I might to put my best foot forward, I can feel my energy is restrained, my attitude is cynical. I go through the motions of doing my job and, thereby, reduce the quality of what I deliver. My clients and students are now suffering as well, and all because we do such a lousy job of taking care of one another.

Until we address our own dysfunctions in the ways we deal with one another, I think it is futile for individual practitioners to keep reading books and attending workshops in the hope that these will help them turn the corner. If only they attended just one more lecture or read one more article, then maybe they would finally leave their doubts and feelings of ineptitude behind.

Sure.

I was certain that if only I got a master's degree in counseling I would finally feel skilled and competent as a professional and human being. That didn't work. Oh, I did learn a few things but my essential feelings of incompetence hardly changed. Then I thought, surely a doctorate would do it. Everyone knows that people with Ph.D.s are supposed to be smart and capable. If there was another degree after a doctorate I would have gone for that as well—with equally dissatisfying results.

No, the answer in finding our way, and helping clients to do the same, has little to do with what we do as individuals to better ourselves. As long as we sabotage one another, fight for our own agendas without consideration for how it affects our colleagues, we are creating as much pain and misery as we purport to eliminate.

We must take a long look at the ways we function as a group of professionals. If we are disrespectful to one another, if we cannot trust each other, if we continue to bicker and undermine one another, we are not the only ones to suffer—so too do the people we are paid to help.

It is time to start applying our skills and knowledge that work so well with client families to our own dysfunctional systems. We should be asking ourselves in meetings the same questions that we ask our clients:

- Wait a minute! What are we really arguing about right now? What is the core issue?
- Who has the power right now and who feels powerless? What does that mean for the ways we are responding to one another?
- How is what we are doing right now helpful to our clients?

- How can we take better care of one another? What can we do to be more supportive?
- In what ways are we acting out? How has our own "family system" in this school or agency become dysfunctional?

The process of finding our way is not a solitary mission; it is a journey that includes our family of origin, our current loved ones, friends and certainly the colleagues with whom we live and work on a daily basis. Until we are willing and able to address how we can do more to help one another feel better about ourselves and what we do, our individual efforts to help clients will ultimately be negated by the damage that is done on a larger scale.

PART IV

Making a
Difference

CHAPTER 18

FIRST CLIENT

Toni DiMargio

Amy wore a halter top and tight blue jeans. Her blonde hair was teased; her expression sassy. Dark blue eye shadow and deep black eyeliner emphasized the feistiness of this petite 15-year-old who had recently attempted suicide. At first glimpse, it appeared she would be difficult to work with.

I approached her prudently, asking our standard first question, "Why do you think you are here?" She squirmed in her seat, never making eye contact, and finally said she wasn't sure. All she knew was that she did *not* want to be where she was! This scenario was all too familiar whenever a new kid was admitted to our adolescent unit. Common reactions included: "What good will this place do me?"; "My mother should be here—she's the one who's nuts!"; "You can't make me do anything I don't want to do."; or "I wish I were dead. I don't care."

As a beginner, I was not ready for such reactions. My graduate school courses dealt with compliant, adult clients who were seeking solace. None of my classes had prepared me for these extraordinary teenagers. I questioned my career choice. How could I possibly help these kids? How could anyone help them? So began a six-month internship that would change my life and those of many young people.

As a teenager, I often rebelled against my parents, and the '60s exaggerated our communication gap. After one year of college, I escaped to California in search of freedom, peace and love. I found street people, drugs and demonstrations (remember People's Park and Vietnam?). Six years later, disillusioned and homesick, I returned to Ohio. After seven more years, I returned to college. Ultimately, in mid-life, I turned the corner to a new career—counseling. So there I was, on the adolescent psychiatric unit, facing teenagers who were most likely rebelling much as I had 20 years earlier.

While my education did not prepare me for these kids, my own experiences did. As I sat across from Amy, probing the surface, I observed a child who appeared frightened and withdrawn. I shared my perceptions and explained that she could set the pace for our session. Though I tried to make eye contact, her gaze drifted away from me. I knew I had to reach her. Desperation might have compelled me to push too fast, but I remembered that clients can only say what they want to say *when* they want to say it.

Patience paid off that first week as it seemed Amy began to trust me. I also began to trust myself. The more Amy revealed to me, the more I relaxed with her. She looked to me for comfort and direction, but I knew I needed that same sense of security. After all, I was new to the counseling profession. Fortunately, I had the opportunity to consult daily with experienced staff on the unit, including psychiatrists, other counselors and my own supervisor. Through them, I found reassurance. When I moved too quickly, I was reminded to be patient. When I hesitated, I was told to follow my intuition tempered by my training.

As Amy's confidence grew, she spoke more openly in both individual and group sessions. She even attempted to counsel some of the other clients!

My self-confidence grew as well. I learned to sit silently, allowing my clients to search for their own words, compose their thoughts and process their emotions. Over time, my sessions with clients became a blend of compassion and fortitude. I pressed, ever so delicately; I retreated, ever so dauntlessly. Their issues often rekindled memories of my own past, allowing each of us to grow, take chances and feel. It didn't matter if we stumbled along the way. We were all too new to this counseling stuff to mind.

When it was time for Amy's discharge, she simply said, "I feel safe here. I don't want to leave." Her sentiments echoed those of most patients on the unit and mine, too. The unit was a place where we all felt safe; a haven from danger, abuse and the unknown. Its structured environment allowed us to know exactly what to expect from day to day, hour to hour, minute to minute. It was a place where emotions could be experienced without trepidation, a place for growing and developing.

As counselors, we prepared these kids for the outside, the real world. Vicariously, we are prepared as well. Amy was discharged. When my internship ended, I was discharged, too. Like Amy, I didn't want to leave. I'm a counselor now, but I will never forget those kids—my first clients—on the unit. They taught me how to be a counselor. They taught me to feel their pain, share their joy and grow as they grew.

Incidentally, I bumped into Amy at the local mall a few weeks ago. She's doing well.

CHAPTER 19

LOST IN THE LAND OF OPPORTUNITY

Don Martin

For the last six years, I have been involved in educational warfare. The combatants experience intense anger, despair, fear and humiliation. They are outcasts in a land of opportunity. Worst of all, they are poor children, children who come to school as young as 5 or 6 and encounter a hostile and threatening environment.

If you want to understand why people burn down sections of Los Angeles and other communities, just take a walk down the hallways of their schools. Children encounter an educational caste system from the first moment they enter school. Their schools are not the same as those of their affluent suburban neighbors or even some of those "white" rural schools outside the city. No, each day these children enter "war-torn" buildings surrounded by low-rent or abandoned housing. You won't find many computers in these schools. In fact, you'll be lucky to find a working bathroom with handles on the faucets.

Whether you live in New York or Oakland, Detroit or Miami, these buildings and their children all look the same—students and teachers look beaten, discouraged and discarded as if they were lumps of coal in the educational furnace.

The words "at-risk" don't even describe these children. They are traumatized. Their lives are like nightmares. Their friends are shot, relatives jailed, and their parents are selling drugs or their bodies to survive. Their meager possessions are stolen by their drug-ravaged and hungry neighbors. While their neighbors in white schools receive a myriad of services and opportunities, these children often are abandoned, even though they face problems their counterparts cannot even comprehend.

Too many of us pretend that what happened in Los Angeles and other communities is a television show that will not be renewed by the local network. I fear that, if what is occurring in our schools does not change soon, our cities will become burning cauldrons and people will have no avenue of escape.

As a member of the civil rights era, I have long been afflicted by optimism and the naive belief that social justice will prevail. I was drawn to counseling because I thought I could make a difference and because I wanted to concentrate less on myself and more on others. I've tried to help people reach their potential, some against difficult odds.

That is why I came back to these schools and these children. Counselors understand and hear the silent cries of people and have the capacity and skills to help. Yet, too many are inadequately trained, overwhelmed and unable or unwilling to provide the services that are needed. Employing one counselor for hundreds of children is a cruel hoax, yet these numbers are more the norm than the exception.

As a counselor educator, I am dismayed that so many of our counselor training programs don't prepare graduates for the real world of inner-city children, whether in schools or community agencies. The lack of minority representation among faculty and students in our counselor education programs has left us without adequate input and vision. Schools needing assistance are within easy reach of many graduate programs, and our training programs need to *involve* students in inner-city schools *throughout* their graduate programs, rather than "placing" a few interns in them during their final semesters.

I have participated in one successful program that develops "on-site" counseling clinics staffed by students, faculty and graduates. The students get excited about providing services to inner-city students and faculty, and about learning all they can about their clients. Public schools are excited that someone cares and wants to help. Our involvement seems to elicit increased community support and provides an opportunity for practicing counselors to donate their time. A few hours a week can make a difference!

No child in our country should have to enter school in fear, surrounded by deficient resources and inadequately trained educators and staff. I believe that significant involvement of counselors in the schools can change this negative and destructive process. "Business as usual" is not good enough anymore. We need to respond to this challenge. We can no longer play the role of outsiders, pretending that someone else will do the work to make our schools respectable.

Certainly, some good work occurs in these schools, and I don't want to offend my colleagues. I know how lonely they are. However, these children need more help! We lose thousands of young people *every day* as more children travel the path to a life of ignorance, despair and poverty than will die of any childhood diseases. This crisis is destroying the core of our country. It is time for a change.

Ultimately, the process of finding your way in the counseling profession involves so much more than pursuing your personal goals or agenda. Each of us has an obligation to make this planet more hospitable and habitable. I have always been impressed by the caring and tenacity exhibited by counseling students in our training programs. I believe that counselor involvement is critical for our profession to make the fundamental changes that must occur in the lives of children.

CHAPTER 20

COUNSELING AT-RISK POPULATIONS: KEEPING THE FAITH

Fred Bemak

Over the years I have met an endless stream of seriously at-risk youth. One client, Jim, was a 16 year old who grew up in a low income family and was severely sexually and physically abused as a child. When I met him, he was so afraid of being hurt that he hadn't let anyone touch or come close to his body for years. To protect himself Jim would aggressively strike out at anyone who violated his self defined one foot "safety zone" which surrounded his body as a buffer from the world. Then there was Susan, a 17 year old who grew up with an angry alcoholic father. Her mother was intermittently physically and emotionally present, leaving Susan at an early age to fend for herself. In Susan's attempts to adapt, she retreated into a fantasy world which grew in scope and magnitude over the years. She had once been popular, but was losing her ability to maintain friends and function in school as the voices became more pronounced. When we finally met, she was very frightened. She explained to me that the voices she heard were getting more insistent and louder.

Somehow Susan and a fifteen year old named John became friends. John's mother had dropped him off on his father's doorstep when he was five years old. He hadn't seen nor heard from his mother in 10 years since she had disappeared, although there were rumors of her living in another state, 1,000 miles away. John was depressed, angry and troubled. No one could even mention "mothers" around John without evoking a strong emotional and physical outburst by this hulking teenager who reacted as if he were still abandoned on that doorstep encased in a lost five year old child's mind. And I still can't forget Bobby, who had witnessed his mother violently killed by his father next to the kitchen table one night. No, he never quite overcame that experience and was having serious problems deciding who he was and adjusting with his peers. Although the magnitude and intensity of the collective and individual stories is overwhelming, each one touches me with concern and compassion and leaves me with questions about how I can help.

Jim, Susan, John and Bobby are representative of my long-standing work with at-risk populations and not so different from the multitudes of other at-risk youth who you know or will meet. I didn't plan this work, never met a colleague who specifically outlined their career goals on the at-risk track, nor found a course during my graduate studies to better train me how to provide counseling for at-risk kids and families. In fact, it seemed like a multi-faceted taboo in the world of graduate training in counseling to discuss issues such as interventions with at-risk youth and families, or poverty, social change and multiculturalism as it related to at-risk populations. Whenever I would raise questions or comments about my everyday reality in graduate classes, there was a clear message that this could warrant "some" discussion but really wasn't within the mainstream of graduate level training. Speaking with other graduate students and professors I quickly realized that almost all of them, at best, could "think" and theorize about the issues but didn't really understand the interrelationship of counseling to such realities as poverty, physical and sexual abuse, racism, hopelessness, rage, substance abuse, multicultural differences or violence. It became apparent that learning would have to come through experience.

Now, 20 years later, I am dismayed at the extent to which this still holds true. Although there is more awareness, concern, discussion and training with regards to at-risk populations, I believe there are major problem areas which persist and present obstacles in our approach to work with at-risk individuals, families, communities and groups. This in turn, affects you and me.

First, most of our graduate programs do not adequately bridge the gap between theory and practice for counseling at-risk clients. We do better at describing at-risk behaviors and problems than defining and exploring effective intervention strategies which are specific to the problem.

Secondly, we haven't fostered a true multidisciplinary approach incorporating professionals who can assist counselors with critical issues such as social, economic, political and health factors relating to interventions for at-risk groups.

A third issue is the lack of integration of multiculturalism with counseling at-risk populations. Although we are now addressing multicultural counseling in a more systematic and thorough manner as compared to two or three decades ago, we still have not researched the interrelationship of cultural diversity, counseling interventions and at-risk populations.

Fourth, graduate programs which address at-risk behaviors and individual, group and family therapeutic interventions frequently offer courses which are independent of the rest of the curriculum, assuming this takes care of training and preparation. What's missing here is a systematic infusion in the curriculum of theory, practice and research applied to at-risk populations.

Finally, it is my experience that we do patchwork training, quick fixes, to try and remedy the deficits of graduate programs. Someone comes into our agency or school to talk about violence, suicide, substance abuse, rape, incest, etc. and spends a few hours or maybe even a day. We may get stimulated, excitely talk about how we might change our clinical work and underlying assumptions about at-risk behaviors and populations, and return to our offices which are loaded with unfinished paperwork and phone messages. Rapidly, our good intentions evaporate and we begin the "catch-up" routine. Given this, I am a strong advocate to eliminate "one shot trainings," and instead develop process oriented long term therapeutic consultation interventions to develop sustained skills, awareness and knowledge and thus *real* change.

My current concern relates to what you and I both hear about the escalating problems of at-risk populations. A drug dealer recently told me that he was prompted to come for counseling only after a *third* friend was shot and killed in his presence. Not the first or second friend—it took *three* for the experience to touch him!

We're seeing this everywhere—more violence, greater rates of physical and sexual abuse, effects of the reconstituted family, socioeconomic pressures, growing feelings of hopelessness and helplessness, a shrinking view of the future, the lack of values or morals, a disregard for others and sanctity of life and the impact of the drug culture. I know many colleagues who feel "disempowered" in their attempts to work with at-risk populations, many of them only admitting their frustrations and limitations privately. One well known and dedicated colleague who has been working for years with at-risk populations surprised me recently when he looked cautiously around to make sure we were alone before quietly commenting, "I don't know . . . maybe we should just give up working here in the city with this {at-risk} population. Maybe I should just go back to writing."

I don't agree. But what do we do? Retreat to some level of more comfortable research? Forget about interventions and the daily struggle of working with "tough" populations. Give up on transforming the quality of university and in-service training? No, despite the problems and difficulties I've encountered with non-compliant and resistant kids, hostile parents and unreachable human services agencies, I have hope. It's true— I still strongly believe that I, and we, can reach each individual, family, school or community. It takes time, effort, lots of energy, fortitude and sustained compassion, but we can do it. Each story of an at-risk child is a life history filled with all the human despair, anger, sadness and pain which goes along with the worst of humanity. Many of these people feel hopeless and without purpose, wondering if another day makes any sense or compassion for others is only a fairytale. Yet I remain firmly convinced that there is hope and assistance. I can honestly say that I have not yet met an at-risk child, adolescent or family who I believed was unreachable. Wounded and hurt, yes; painstakingly difficult to reach, yes; testing patience, yes; pushing limits, yes; making me angry and frustrated, sure; impossible to find some glimmer of hope, humanity, care and a desire to heal, a place to be touched, no.

With the shifting dynamics of problems and corresponding paradigms which will effectively address these concerns, we must be diligent in committing ourselves to the process of change. Trial and error, courage to admit our own inabilities and limits, collaboration with other exploring professionals—these are crucial to our journey. I also think we must take risks, facilitate serious change to challenge the mainstream of the universities where we teach and learn, as well as the agencies, schools and programs where we work daily. We must confront these places to reconceptualize how to address the mental health at-risk populations of the future, discarding old habits and constructs which no longer work. Without this role as leaders and change agents with our systems, I'm afraid that the growing number of Jim's, Susan's, John's and Bobby's of the world will stagnate in pacification mental health stability programs, totally losing all hope. We in the counseling field have been in some respects the bearers of hope. Let's not develop our own class system for "at-risk" and "non at-risk." I guess I would just say: "Keep on keeping the faith."

CHAPTER 21

BEYOND RESEARCH AND WORKSHOPS IS THE MAGICAL POWER OF HELPING PEOPLE

Jeffrey A. Kottler

We have no words to describe adequately the dimensions of power implicit in the counseling process. We speak of influence, modeling, persuasion, but none of these concepts does justice to the almost magical transformation that takes place between a professional helper and a client.

We know there are certain skills, personality traits and behaviors associated with promoting change in others. Whether we are looking at effective politicians, coaches or counselors, we might use the term charisma to describe their ability to influence people through the force and spirit of their personalities.

My whole professional life I have been searching for the words to describe how learning in general, and counseling in particular, takes place. I have been dissatisfied with the often parochial and compartmentalized ways that we go about trying to make sense of this complex interchange between client and counselor. In the journey to find my way, whether as a beginner or veteran, I have been seeking to find the essence behind what we do. Why is it that what some may do with their clients seems to be so different from what others would do? How can we favor such a variety of counseling approaches and emphasize such diverse principles of counseling, and yet still be comparably effective?

I just completed a supervision session with a beginning counselor who was told by her previous mentor that she should end every session by prescribing homework assignments. She found this worked remarkably well motivating her clients to put the discussions from their sessions into action, but I was aghast at the rigidity of this procedure: "It's fine to build homework into your counseling," I told her, "but people are far more committed to completing tasks if they come up with them on their own (or believe they have) rather than having you tell them what to do. Don't worry so much in these first sessions about getting things done; build a supportive relationship first."

My style of supervision and practice could not have been more different than this counselor's previous mentor. Whereas he emphasized cognitive/behavioral dimensions, I was stressing an equal share of the affective domain. While he stressed a defensible plan of action and specific interventions, I was supporting a more flexible method of responding to client needs at any moment in time. Yet in spite of this approach that contradicted many of the things she had heard previously, I could find no evidence that my way was necessarily better than the one she had been using before. In the end, I told her, the key is to find your own way.

In other chapters I have contemplated whether our different approaches are really so different after all. Maybe we just *appear* to do different things but there is a central core to all effective counseling. Among these universal ingredients that underlie the counseling process is the personal power of the helper.

I know that there is something about the counselor as a person that makes a tremendous difference in the way things progress. I know that in my own experiences as a client, student and intern I have been less impressed by what mentors have said than by *how* they said it. There was something about their confidence, their exuberance in what they were doing, their faith in me and the power that seemed to vibrate from their inner core, that kept me spellbound. I was open to what they offered because I liked and respected them as people, as well as professionals.

I have read about certain attitudes like acceptance and unconditional regard. I have observed in videos and demonstrations of prominent practitioners, as well as the sessions of counselors I supervise, that something powerful takes place between people beyond any techniques or interventions that are employed. There is something about the personal power of the helper that motivates, inspires, soothes and supports the client. I have felt at a loss, however, to use the concepts available in our field to describe what is taking place. I have been searching for the right words that preserve the complexity and magic of the change process.

It was while working with several native Maori colleagues in New Zealand that I was introduced to a few of the basic themes that are part of this ancient Polynesian culture. There are two words, in particular, that seemed so relevant to what we do. After years of struggling to describe what transpires when one person in a position of power and authority influences another who seeks help, I came across two words embedded in Maori culture that capture the essence of what we do. *Ihi* is the magnetic presence and psychic force that is part of all humans, but is especially powerful in teachers and healers. Ihi inspires awe, respect and even a kind of apprehension.

If ihi refers to psychic power, then *mana* encompasses its spiritual companion. Descended from the gods as a kind of lawful permission to act on their behalf, mana represents sanctioned authority from another source to influence others. Together, both ihi and mana refer to the psychological/spiritual power that we often think of as charisma. This is what attracts clients to us, maintains their interest and excitement, opens them up to possibilities within themselves and the world around them. We could be the most brilliant thinkers and wise counselors in the universe, yet without the ihi and mana to generate awe in others, nobody will even pay attention to what we have to say.

I wonder now about the ways we seek to train ourselves as counselors, to improve our effectiveness as helpers. Hungry for new knowledge, we devour books and articles. Finding our way through a maze of confusion, we attend lectures and workshops to learn new skills and incorporate the latest therapeutic strategies into our repertoire. But if ihi and mana are truly the source of our power to influence others, I wonder what we are doing to develop these capacities? How do we go about becoming more psychologically and spiritually forceful? And how do we do so while maintaining a sense of restraint, integrity and moral responsibility so that this power is not abused?

One other Maori concept that might offer some guidance in the use of ihi and mana is *tapu*. This is the realm of the "sacred righteousness" described in the Old Testament or the New Testament's "moral righteousness." Tapu is both a religious and legal term that suggests a contractual relationship between client and counselor that is untouchable in its purity. It is sacred in the sense that counselors vow to dedicate themselves to serve others, to use their ihi and mana only for selfless good. Any transgression of moral purity would be sacrilegious, breaking the law of tapu, violating the source of mana and ihi.

I now believe that in the journey to find my way as a counselor, as well as helping others to do so, there is so much more than reading books and articles, attending lectures and workshops, participating in supervision and staff meetings, developing skills and expertise. There is also the greater challenge of recognizing our own ihi and mana, developing these attributes of our personal power in such a way that we honor the tapu, or the sacred obligation to use our influence for the good of clients and the world at large.

If ihi and mana are not something we do, but something we *are*, then it is not a matter of turning ourselves on and off when the "meter" is running. It is our acts of kindness and compassion throughout our lives, not only at the office but at the market or on the street, not only with our clients and family but with our colleagues, that build the force of our power to help others.

PART V

REFINING OUR THINKING

CHAPTER 22

IMITATING, INTEGRATING AND IMPLEMENTING

Jeffrey A. Kottler

Graduate school was often confusing for me, as it was for most of my peers. I felt so much pressure from my professors and supervisors to do well; but most of all, I put pressure on myself.

I wrestled with questions that are often at the forefront of so many students' and beginning counselors' minds. Do I have what it takes to be a counselor? Am I bright enough and talented enough to learn all these complicated theories, master the core of counseling skills and somehow put it all together in such a way that I can ever help someone? I hope that some of my personal answers to these questions will help others in their transition from being a beginner to becoming a seasoned professional.

Each week I would sit awestruck, watching my professors in action. Some of them always seemed to know exactly what they were doing. They had an answer for everything. They would present amazingly complex cases, describing the client's pain and symptoms, the configurations of their behavior, their defenses and games. They would proceed to describe how they knew just what was going on with this particular client, which buttons needed to be pushed and what interventions were needed. Voila! The person was cured.

We would watch films in our classes of the masters demonstrating their craft. It was not unusual that in a single-hour session, the theorist would interview a client, diagnose the presenting complaints (as well as underlying issues), implement some wonderful treatment program that would effect startling changes and still save 15 minutes to describe what he or she did and why it worked. Usually this explanation was some variation of the message: "What I do works far better than what everyone else is doing, and if you really want to practice effective counseling you should be like me."

Needless to say, after watching my professors in action and seeing the masters on film, I began to feel more and more overwhelmed. How was I ever going to learn all this great stuff? Now that I was seeing real clients, how could I ever attend to their concerns while I was trying to stay consistent with the theoretical model I was practicing?

The problem was compounded by the perplexing phenomenon that many of my professors, supervisors and mentors seemed to be extremely effective practicing counseling, *even though they did such different things*. I watched Carl Rogers work his wonders with caring, compassion and empathy. I wanted to crawl into his lap, have him hug me and tell me everything would be all right. I imitated him and memorized his lines and style. I wanted to be just like him. Observing Albert Ellis apply his craft, I was stunned with the power of his interventions. For months afterwards, I imitated his voice, his jokes, his irreverence. I even applied his theory to several ongoing cases and noticed some immediate improvement. Clearly this also was the kind of counselor I wanted to be.

I bounced around like a ping pong ball during my early years moving from one mentor to another, seeking an authority figure to give me the approval and validation I longed for. Who would reassure me that I was indeed talented and had potential? I found that the best way to win these accolades and to have professors and supervisors like me, was to try my best to be like them. Once I embraced a particular style or theory modeled by a mentor, I felt more secure and less confused—that is, until I met someone else who seemed just as effective doing something radically different.

It took much reflection to initially figure out how it was possible for so many experts to be so effective while they *appeared* to do such different things. It seems that you can help people by confronting them or nurturing them; that you can focus on feelings, thoughts *or* behaviors; that you can talk a little or a lot; that you can be rational, intuitive, analytic, spontaneous, controlled, deliberate or irreverent and still be a good counselor.

What seems to make the most difference in helping clients is *not* which theory is practiced, but how comfortable you are adapting your own personality and style of practice to the particular client's needs and specific counseling situation. What my best professors, mentors, supervisors and heroes all had in common was that they shared some basic attributes and values. They were passionate, confident, moral and extremely competent individuals. Most of all, they truly believed in what they were doing.

Once I stopped trying so hard to imitate everyone else, I realized that there are so many different ways to apply the core of knowledge, skills and research in individually designed ways. I began to feel a lot less pressure. Don't misunderstand me: I am *still* confused much of the time trying to figure out how and why this wonderful process of counseling works. But I no longer believe there is a single correct way to operate.

One of the most basic values of our profession is helping clients find their own path to growth and change. Beginning counselors have the opportunity to apply this important principle to their own lives. The ultimate goal of training and development as a counselor is to create a personal style of practice consistent with current knowledge, research and ethical standards that is compatible with the strengths of one's unique personality and experiences.

Rather than seeking an inflexible system in which you subjugate yourself in the process of trying to become like a mentor, you can take a more challenging path. The task of finding your own way means integrating the best of *every* teacher and supervisor you have ever had. It means blending *everything* that you have read about and seen modeled in your classes into a framework that is uniquely your own.

Perhaps the greatest benefit of this profession is that it not only allows but also encourages us to apply what we do with our clients to our own lives. Most of all, this means staying open to all that you experience and observe, evaluating critically what you see as most effective and making the best parts of all your mentors the best parts of you.

Chapter 23

Discovering
What You Believe

Gerald Corey

Beginning a helping career isn't easy—in fact, it can involve a great deal of anxiety and uncertainty. Such was the case for me.

At the beginning of my career as a counselor, I wasn't very confident. Even though I was teaching full-time and counseling only part-time, I went through a period of doubt over whether to do any counseling at all. I wondered if it would be better to stick to teaching and forget about any aspirations of counseling others—particularly disconcerting because I had just completed a doctorate in counseling.

When I began practicing at a university counseling center, I frequently wondered what I could do for my clients. I often had no idea of what, if anything, my clients were getting from our sessions. I couldn't tell if they were getting better, staying the same or getting worse. It was important to me that all my clients like me, think well of me and that they showed progress by making changes.

What I didn't know at the time was that clients need to struggle to find their own answers. I wanted them to feel better quickly, for then I would know that I was surely a help to them. What I didn't realize was that clients often feel worse as they give up their defenses and open themselves to their pain.

When I saw clients expressing their fear and uncertainty about their future, it only brought out my own doubt that I could help them. Giving my clients the appropriate responses to their statements was of utmost importance, but I was so concerned about saying the wrong thing that I listened too much and didn't give enough reaction. When I did give a response, I frequently found myself thinking, "How would my supervisor say this? Can I help everyone who comes to my office? What can I do or say to clients who feel depressed and stuck? Do I really know enough and have enough skill to be effective?"

By asking these questions, I burdened myself with the expectation that I should be all things to all people, that although the feelings of hopelessness my clients expressed made me uncomfortable, I saw it as my role to motivate them and alleviate their depression.

It seemed that most clients were "difficult customers" in one way or another and that if I were more talented, I would reach them. These clients, who seemed to make very few changes, were the ones who increased my own anxiety. But rather than seeing them as responsible in part for their progress or lack of it, I blamed myself for not knowing enough and not being able to solve their problems. I took full responsibility for what they did during the session. My self-doubts grew when they did not show up for following appointments. I was sure that this was a sign that they were dissatisfied with what they were getting from me. It never occurred to me that this behavior might have said something about them and their unwillingness to change.

I had limited tolerance for uncertainty and my clients' struggles to find their own direction. To be sure, many of these clients sought counseling with the expectation that they would find simple solutions to their problems. If their expectations were not met, they were likely to view me as being less than competent. It took me some time to teach clients that the therapeutic process is a joint venture and that a counselor can best function as a guide, not as an expert who has all the answers for them.

I particularly remember encouraging depressed clients to see one of the other counselors on the staff. Working with depressed clients was difficult for me because of my own fear of depression. This experience taught me that I could not take clients in any direction that I was not willing to explore myself.

I don't think we ever arrive at a place where there is nothing new to learn. Although I hope that we can be humble, we shouldn't put ourselves down for all that we don't know. Counselors don't have to be perfect—in fact, they shouldn't be, or our clients who see themselves as far from perfect will not learn from us. My experience has taught me that expecting perfection from ourselves only serves to keep us stuck.

It's essential that we are there for our clients, that we are centered within ourselves and that we listen to ourselves as well as our clients. If we can respond openly to our clients by letting them know how they are affecting us, we can do much more for them than if we burden ourselves with trying to come up with the perfect intervention.

By becoming obsessed with saying exactly the "right" thing, we remove ourselves from the person who seeks our guidance. When we free ourselves from the restrictions of being the perfect professional, we can tap into our creativity and truly be ourselves as we work with clients.

One way that we can become freer is to stop the internal rehearsals that tend to be self-defeating. For example, once we realize that we are too critical of ourselves, we can learn to lighten up. Once we identify the voice inside us that makes us feel guilty, less than competent or that we have failed, we can stop it. Indeed, we can create a new voice if we are willing to work at this process.

I encourage my students to keep a journal to record their thoughts, feelings and actions. It is an excellent tool for recognizing the ways we often sabotage ourselves.

It's also helpful to focus on your own reactions, rather than those of your clients. What are our clients teaching us about ourselves? What can we learn about our own unfinished business by paying attention to the clients we consider "difficult?" How can clients be a mirror for us and how can we see ourselves as we really are? My hope is that beginning counselors will seek teachers of all sorts and allow themselves the freedom to keep on learning.

CHAPTER 24

COUNSELING IS A MULTIPLE-CHOICE TEST

Paul Jones

More than a few years have passed since my rites of passage from graduate school to actual practice (for reference, sex was safe, and Hondas were small motor scooters). I think it is important that we each retain vivid memories of the combined fear and excitement of flying "mentorless" in our chosen profession.

One of my colleagues recently suggested that the transition from practica to actual practice is easier if you recognize that counseling in real life is "not a multiple-choice test." He noted that frequently you will be confronted with questions that have no apparent best answer. The "correct" answer would often be disputed among the experienced professionals with whom you have trained.

Soon after that publication, the author and I were exchanging barbs (not an uncommon activity between good friends), about whether life can/should actually be framed as a multiple-choice test. That banter led to more serious dialogue about the underlying issue involved, and ultimately inspires this piece.

My colleague claimed that if a group of supervisors were faced with the same case, they would likely make widely disparate suggestions to a counselor on how to proceed. My own experience with professional counselors, however, suggests the opposite. I find, instead, a remarkable similarity in the approach to planning and delivering counseling services.

My belief is based on experience that comes from a career path that defies placement in a developmental model. In what my friends are allowed to define as a checkered career, I have moved from school counselor, to test maker, to university administrator, to private practitioner, to university faculty (and I'm really not that old). Counselor education programs are offered in my department, but my course assignments (with the periodic exception of an appraisal course), are in educational psychology, and my research interest is in rehabilitation.

Such a history places acknowledged limitation on my understanding of the role of counselor educator. I have observed, more than participated in, counselor education. My background has provided me extensive opportunity to work in varied settings with practitioners trained in different disciplines with divergent models.

The similarity and frequent consensus among those practitioners is striking. For example, in treatment team meetings conducted in inpatient psychiatric hospitals, the professional counselor, the psychologist, the social worker and the psychiatrist often have quite different views about the etiology of a client's distress. But when planning for intervention, they tend to identify similar client needs, goals and intervention procedures. When a counseling session is evaluated for effectiveness, similar feedback is often given regardless of a practitioner's professional identification. One psychiatrist with whom I worked made the insightful comment, "it looks like we went to different schools, together."

While my experience has been varied, it is hardly unique. I believe that you will encounter the phenomenon of similarity whether your practice is in a school, a public agency or a private setting. Active practitioners from different disciplines exhibit common beliefs. Few care which "model" you use. All are concerned about whether your intervention was successful. If my premise is correct, there is a challenge here for both the counselor educator and the newly minted professional counselor.

My position clearly suggests the belief that the independent variable is whether the person offering an opinion is engaged in active practice. Those actually delivering counseling services appear to develop similar beliefs and patterns of behavior in service delivery. Those who may doubt this are challenged to escape the ivory tower and spend time in the arena where real services are provided to real people. The emphasis (overemphasis) on differences in counseling approaches is symptomatic of those who are not engaged in active practice. Although this is not intended as just a replay of "those who can, do; those who can't, teach," I do believe that counselor education faculties are replete with examples of "those who can, don't."

I challenge my university colleagues in counselor education to consider investing more time in demonstrating effective intervention and less time in talking about it. Acknowledging that the term "medical model" can be a dirty phrase, we may have something to learn from the medical profession's history of education for intervention. In addition to the requisite text-based content, medical students learn to practice medicine on their own, in part, by observing how trained physicians deal with actual cases. How long has it been since you, the counselor educator, invited a student to observe your work in an ongoing case with a client?

In actual practice, shared work with clients is frequent. Consider the impact if in beginning practicum, the supervisor and the student were to be co-therapists for each client, making the student a participant observer in the process. Viewing a tape by one of the "masters" is hardly a substitute for active participation in the drama of intervention with a real client. From the other side, the typical procedure now employed in which the supervisor views a video of student and client does not allow for the recognition of nuances that are often critical in actual intervention. (And the process must be incredibly boring to the supervisor, who in many instances, might easily be replaced by a computer programmed with speech capabilities.)

Carl Rogers may have overestimated in identifying conditions as necessary "and sufficient," but the similarity among experienced practicing professional counselors suggests that there must be a few critical elements that actually define effective counseling. I believe that practicing counselors find focus on such elements, and that counselor educators actually delivering services would tend to do likewise.

It's easier to focus attention on the differences in counseling approaches, especially among the different disciplines. We boast that our work is based on a developmental model emphasizing prevention in a way that sometimes suggests that psychologists and social workers rejoice in societal illness and have never heard of Piaget. The family systems advocates among us sometimes make it appear as if those with differing orientations never consider the importance of work with a family unit. The question is not whether there are differences but whether those differences are actually important.

Having vented these feelings, I'd like to offer some of my own suggestions to those about to embark on a career in professional counseling. First, if my thoughts about counselor education seem valuable, you are in the position to make it happen. In the university setting, we change slowly; first we assign the problem to a committee. Change in the training models is more likely if the stimulus comes from the practicing professionals.

I also would suggest that you avoid anticipating a battle with other professionals about how to work with a person in need. Your differences more likely involve vocabulary than appropriate action. Although the "correct" vocabulary was an essential skill to get you through graduate school, it will buy you little in the real world. There certainly are important differences among practicing professionals, but I believe that they involve competence and incompetence, not theory, model or discipline. In actual practice you often will be faced with a "multiple-choice question." Given the available choices, what should you do next with this client? The most competent clinician in your first work setting may be a social worker, rather than a professional counselor. I suggest that you model that person's behavior, regardless of their identified discipline.

Finally, welcome to the community. You have, without question, selected the most exciting, challenging and personally rewarding career available. I wish you well.

CHAPTER 25

DIAGNOSTIC DISORDER WITH LABELING FEATURES

Mark Schorr

Most commonly seen in beginning therapists, DDLF is character-
ized by a passionate clutching of the Diagnostic and Statistical Manual
(DSM-IV), a tendency to slap on labels quicker than a supermar-
ket stock clerk and a desire to feel safe by pigeonholing any client.

Throughout training, counselors are given conflicting messages when it comes to diagnostic labels. We know that every client is an individual with unique problems. Labeling clients can have serious consequences—we might come to see them only as "borderlines," "bipolars" or "narcissists." And if clients ever learned their labels, they might be more inclined to act the part.

On the other hand, many of us were taught to consult the DSM IV the way theology students refer to the Bible. Professors emphasized the nuances and subtle differences among diagnostic distinctions. "What are the differences between a schizoaffective client and a bipolar client in a manic phase with psychotic features?" "What is the relationship between dysthymia and major depression?" "Could a client be histrionic, or that favorite label for difficult clients, a borderline?"

Using diagnostic labels so casually can replace the person. You cease to think of your client as John Doe, a man suffering from borderline personality disorder. Instead Doe becomes a "borderline" or the more terse "BPD." Your colleagues know exactly what you mean.

But diagnostic labels are also necessary to communicate quickly and efficiently with colleagues. When I meet with my supervisor, it is much easier to rattle off a label and a few key DSM IV criteria than to explain the specifics of my client's troubled life.

Diagnostic labels must be used to placate the great god of third-party payments. The importance of coverage was made clear to me early on when I briefed a colleague on a client. "What's her Axis Six status?" he asked. Seeing my ignorant expression, he said, "Axis Six. Funding."

In school, I must admit, playing diagnostician was fun. Cases were presented and I had to use fledgling clinical powers to deduce the disorder, a challenge as intriguing as a hot game of Clue or Trivial Pursuit.

But when real people sat before me and I nervously sifted through the tragic details of their lives, the game was not quite as amusing. Should I go with a minimal diagnosis, applying the least offensive label? Or should I go for a label that would guarantee them more extensive treatment? And what about Axes Four and Five—quantifying the client's level of functioning, their level of suffering—where the diagnosis was really a judgment call?

One of my first clients was diagnosed with depression and post-traumatic stress disorder. She was classified as an Axis One client because these problems are usually less complicated than other disorders. But it was all but impossible to keep this client focused during our sessions. There were indications of entitlement issues, manipulativeness, self-serving stories, poor impulse control and difficulty in developing a therapeutic relationship. When she tried to get me to give her a calendar off the wall, I realized that there was a lot more going on.

My first reaction was to label her as antisocial. But what had made her so alienated and desperate? Her life was a complete mess.

She seemed to get better during therapy, even though she missed nearly half her appointments and came late or brought her boyfriend's child to the other sessions. When I tried setting rules, backed by the threat of termination, she pleaded that I was the only one she could talk to.

She needed a caring person to relate to, not someone who would lump her into convenient categories. Rather than seeing her as a sophisticated and cunning adversary, I saw her as a somewhat selfish kid, robbed of her childhood by physical and sexual abuse.

Eventually she dropped out of treatment and disconnected her phone. But at last report, she had joined Alcoholics Anonymous, was involved with a non-abusive boyfriend and had evicted a substance-abusing housemate. The antisocial label still fit, but her problems had become more personal. She was no longer a list of criteria, a number, a brand. She had become a genuine person in pain.

As I proceeded through my internship, I fell into a classic beginner's mistake. Rather than label, I described. Unfortunately, there is no time to write detailed accounts of every client. More and more often I hurry to apply a label, a diagnostic shorthand that I hope other therapists can understand.

Deciding whether to apply a diagnostic label means asking yourself, am I doing this to benefit myself, or to benefit the client? Am I calling the client a borderline to cover my own fears or to help explain their problems? Do I label them obsessive-compulsive because it will help in developing treatment or because it allows me to write them off?

Counselors try to balance severity of diagnosis with need for treatment, our own biases with the system's demands, the desire for humanity with the concern for numbers. It's confusing. Perhaps that's symptomatic of DDLF.

CHAPTER 26

ETHICAL CODES AND RESPONSIBLE DECISION-MAKING

Wayne Lanning

One of the many concerns beginning counselors face is making appropriate ethical decisions. The reality of professional practice is that we generally can't solve dilemmas by applying what we learned in our ethics classes.

Ethics are defined as a set of philosophical beliefs about the way things should be. Counseling ethics are professional beliefs (and accompanying statements) about the way things ought to be in the counseling profession. But simply learning the ethical codes and casebooks will not prepare someone for a career or ethical practice. Almost nothing in the codes is identified as absolutely wrong. (An exception is the prohibition against having sex with clients.) The codes give us principles—such as keeping confidentiality and developing trust, promoting the welfare of clients and refraining from interfering with the effective work of a professional colleague—upon which ethical counseling is based.

The problem counselors face is determining what to do when faced with a dilemma—what occurs when, no matter what we decide, we may violate some ethical principle.

I believe that more important than knowing the code, or even the principles contained in the code, is to understand the ethical and moral principles that we hold as individual professional counselors. We will likely share many of these principles with most of our professional colleagues. They will include those learned from professors and supervisors and fellow students, and those adopted from involvement in the profession. But not all of the principles professed by ACA or its divisions are principles with which we all agree.

Some new counseling professionals may disagree with popular principles of the profession because some of those principles conflict with their personal belief system. The most consistent struggle beginning counselors have is between a value that supposedly represents a principle of the profession but conflicts with their personal ethical or moral belief system. For example, the codes are very clear that "the primary obligation of the member is to respect the integrity and promote the welfare of the client(s)." But what does that mean? Does that mean we *should* promote the client's self-determination and independence from the controls of others, including family? Many would say yes, but some believe strongly in the culture of parental and extended family approval for making decisions. Then, is it in the client's best interest to promote self-determination?

So how do we make a decision in the midst of so much apparent confusion? In the words of Fred Friendly from the series on "Ethics in America": "Our purpose is not to make up anyone's mind but to open minds and to make the agony of the decision-making so intense that you can escape only by thinking." The most difficult part of being a professional counselor is having to make decisions when we will be responsible for the consequences. That is a lonely task. But we can manage it if we use a systematic process of ethical reasoning.

Ethical reasoning is the process of determining which ethical principles are involved and then prioritizing them based on the professional requirements and personal beliefs. Never pretend that counselors agree on most of the principles in life. That is why we have members of our profession on both sides of such issues as abortion, capital punishment, the military, saving the whales, trophy hunting and dozens of other issues that involve personal beliefs about the way things "should" be in the world.

To reason through a situation, first identify the professional ethical principles involved. There will be many and even those that seem simple frequently won't be. For example, is a dual relationship present if you write a letter of reference for a client? What appears to be a simple answer to that question becomes more complicated when we apply the process of ethical reasoning. Some principles involved in that question include promoting the welfare of the client, confidentiality of information received in counseling and the inequality of a counselor/client relationship. Careful consideration of all principles within the context of the specific situation may well lead a counselor to conclude that writing a letter for a client who is seeking admission to graduate school places the counselor in a position of advocacy for the client that is beyond the scope of what a counselor/client relationship "should" be. But the important thing to remember is that the process of reasoning must place some principles in a position of more importance than others. Confidentiality is not an absolute ethical principle in counseling. If it were,

112

then it could not be "violated" when there is imminent danger of harm to self or others. Other exceptions also apply but can only be identified when one has reasoned through the individual dilemma being faced.

Remember that the decision one counselor makes when facing a dilemma may not be the same one that an equally ethical professional counselor reaches. That is what makes being a professional so difficult at times. We can consult with our colleagues, call an ethics professor, read the ethics books, and more; but when we make the final decision, it is ours alone. We alone are responsible and accountable for the consequences. Nevertheless, the ability to reason with the ethical principles and arrive at a decision for which we are willing to be accountable is what makes a counseling practice ethical. That is a difficult but not impossible task and one that in many ways determines the level of our professionalism.

PART VI

RECOGNITION AND SELF-PROMOTION

CHAPTER 27

TOOTING YOUR HORN

Stuart Sobel

Do all counselors need weight reduction programs? Sometimes, when I go to meetings and I look around it feels that way. It's really no secret as to why many of us are overweight. When I visit guidance departments in various schools, I'm immediately surrounded by baked goods. There's Joan's ricotta pie. There's Ellen's apple-nut pound cake. There's Patricia's Barbados fruit cake. As I stuff rugelach into my mouth I'm participating in a department feeding frenzy. A school of piranha fish has nothing on our gang.

I have wondered why we are doing this. The answer that comes to my mind is that we must be rewarding ourselves. And why not? Nobody else does! It seems that it is a rare occasion when anyone tells us that we are doing a good job. As I look over my career as a counselor, I wonder how I found my way and succeeded in a work situation where there was little positive feedback and little on-the-job training.

As a new counselor, I wanted validation. I realized that I and many of my colleagues were warmed by approval and responded with energy and devotion. Without that external validation, for many of us our work was in danger of becoming a non-event.

I've been in job situations where the only time I was aware I had a supervisor was when I was summoned to explain what was perceived as an error I had made. This was in a school where my colleagues told me that as long as administration seemed to be ignoring my presence on staff I was to assume they were pleased. As far as I'm concerned this is wrong. To be a rose blooming unseen in a garden certainly never did anything for my morale. I think that as mental health providers we want someone we respect to congratulate us, praise us, recommend us for an award, and if it's a supervisor, write us a note for the file that acknowledges some contribution we've made. We want to know that the work we're doing is appreciated and valued. This is not to say that many counselors are not self motivated. In situations where there is little positive interaction, they would have to be self starters. In my opinion, these are work sites that are not good environments for new counselors.

When the New York City Board Of Education began to give an annual award to one counselor from each superintendency in the city, I attended the award ceremonies. Entire families were present with cameras, flowers, and other gifts to recognize the moment. The glow coming from the counselors receiving the plaques that were distributed was only surpassed by the radiance emanating from their loved ones. For a counselor to be recognized was so rare, so unusual, that this receiving of a plaque took on tremendous meaning. Too many counselors only speak to the principal when summoned to discuss a perceived error in judgment the counselor made. The meeting is usually initiated by a parent complaint. The interaction is a negative one. My belief is that in too many schools the powers-that-be pay lip service to the work of the counselor, but haven't really internalized the good things counselors do on a daily basis.

Early in my career, I became the second licensed guidance counselor in a large urban senior high school. I was given the title of omnibus counselor (he who does everything the administration can't find anyone else to do) and was assigned to be the only counselor in the school's ninth grade annex. I was to service an incoming class of approximately 600 students. At the end of each day, my supervisor expected me in his office. He would call for my interview cards and literally weigh them in his hand. If there wasn't a hefty feel there was a question as to how I had spent my day. He respected confidentiality enough not to read the cards, but weigh them he did. The fact that working with three severely disturbed students can eat your soul, while telling an assembly of students that English 2 follows English 1 won't drain your energies did not impress him. The numbers had to be there. As a counselor, what can we do in this kind of a situation?

I solved my problem by educating him. He was bright. However, he knew that I had no classes, no hall patrol, no lunch duty, no official class responsibilities and no disciplinary work. How could I possibly be spending my day? So, on a regularly scheduled basis, usually at the end of the day weigh-in time, I shared with him the day's triumphs and tragedies. Whether I needed it or not, I made sure to ask his advice on matters I thought he could answer. In all honesty I came to appreciate his feedback. The important thing was that in getting his advice, and following it when appropriate, *I bonded him to the effort*. I had found an intelligent professional in a position of authority who I could talk to about problems I was encountering. Of course, when it came to improving my methodology in being a counselor, I turned to those who had training in this area. If I had known it existed, I would have sought out paid supervision. However, for matters that required good common sense, and a sharp mind from someone not directly involved in the problem, he was there for me.

What I'm suggesting to beginning mental health providers is that you do something similar. You have to be your own public relations agent. Not only will it help you, it will help the department and the profession. Don't wait to be noticed and recognized. Don't think it's unseemly to boast about your triumphs. It doesn't break confidentiality to tell a supervisor that a certain child is functioning today because of your work with him. It's not wrong to volunteer to speak at a faculty conference about the work of the counselor. It's not wrong to plan and to implement a series of guidance related conferences directed towards parents or to speak at department meetings about your work and how it affects the staff. I believe that all members of the school family have an obligation to educate the rest of the school about their work.

So what is our message?

1. We're the ones who do conflict resolution with one result being that the headlines of the local newspaper don't scream about the lack of safety in our school.
2. We do crisis intervention. I remember one school where there was a completed student suicide. There was a danger of other students doing the same thing, but the work of the crisis response counselors prevented this from happening. I made sure that the staff and the administration knew what a great job the mental health providers had done and what they had been spared because of the work of the guidance staff.
3. We're the ones who call the hotline to make sure that the child gets needed help and to make sure that the school can't be accused of looking the other way when an incident occurs.
4. We see to it that a student has a program that leads to graduation so that a justifiably irate parent isn't creating a public scene because a student is missing one credit that will bar him from tomorrow's ceremonies.
5. We personalize programs so that a student and a teacher with dramatically opposed personalities don't have to sit in the same room glaring at each other for one or two terms.
6. We find the one thing in the school day that keeps the potential dropout in attendance and then we make sure it's on his program.
7. We find the colleges or the entry level jobs that seem to be good matches for our students.
8. We prepare students and their families for therapy when indicated.

Of course, you can add to the list. And we know that we don't do all of these things on a daily basis, but we do enough to make a significant contribution to school life.

It is our responsibility, in a planned and purposeful way, to let the rest of the school family know that our work makes their work lives flow more easily.

So, dear colleagues, it's not enough to drown our feelings of being taken for granted in the cookie bowl. It's time we embarked on our own weight control program. This is a program that uses our abilities to communicate to publicize the positive things that we do. Our efforts can begin with talks at parent, department and school-wide meetings on how our work facilitates the work of our colleagues, a guidance department newsletter that tells the school community what we're about, and an open channel of communication to the principal to make him or her part of our team.

If we want to be appreciated, we have to let people know that they have something to appreciate. To paraphrase Gilbert and Sullivan, we must blow our own trumpets.

Let the music begin.

CHAPTER 28

BECOMING FAMOUS

Melinda Lewis Merrigan

One day, a colleague and I were discussing "observations" of children. I was telling her how difficult it was for me to observe a child at recess that day, because so many other children were coming up to me for hugs and a hello. She said to me, "Well, that's because you're famous!" We laughed, but reflecting on her comment later I realized she was right. I am "famous" with the children at our school. It's what keeps me busy and it's also what helps me do the best possible job I can.

Although I am writing about finding my way as a school counselor, there are implications to "being famous" in any counseling setting. Children get to know me easily, and if there is a need for help the rapport is more easily developed. Children at our school want to spend time with me. They know they will find a friendly, caring person who will try to help them work things out. Being famous can give you more opportunities to connect with children, teachers and other professionals. Colleagues may feel more comfortable stopping in to talk with you, referring a child to you or even asking for advice if they are given the chance to get to know who you are and what you do.

One way I have become famous is by taking the time to be visible to children, parents and staff. The children see me in places other than my office. I get involved in schoolwide events and make an effort to go on at least one field trip a year. I greet the children in the morning when they come to school, and I am there when they leave. Sometimes you need to leave that pile of paperwork behind and just get out and roam the halls. Visit the playground at recess time occasionally. Go into classrooms just to be with the kids. Get involved in projects they are working on. Let the children, as well as your colleagues, know you're around.

Every year I set up a time with each teacher to visit their classroom during the first week of school. I spend 15 to 30 minutes introducing myself and letting the students know what I do as the school counselor. (Agency counselors could attempt the same kind of public relations outreach in their community.) Although many students know me well after their first year in the school, it is a good refresher for them and allows any new students to get a glimpse of what's available for them. One of my happiest memories is of the time I overheard one student point me out to her little sister and say, "That's Mrs. Merrigan. She's the school's problem solver."

Sometimes children just need a little extra attention to get them through the school day. I have found that it's important for children to know that I'm available for a hug and a smile anytime they need one. I walk down the halls and have students come up for a hug or just a "highfive." I always hear someone saying, "Hi, Mrs. Merrigan," and I always say, "Hi," back to them. I have made a real effort to learn students' names and use them when saying hello. Sometimes the smallest gesture of recognition can mean the world to a child who is having a hard day. When making out a schedule, I always leave some flexible time in each day. This allows me to fit in a session with that boy who didn't sleep last night because his parents had been fighting, or the two girls who absolutely have to see me today, because they used to be best friends and just had a fight.

Whether you work in an elementary or secondary school, or in a community agency, try to find a way to connect with those who use your services. I find that my day is filled with crises of all shapes and sizes and that the students I spend the most time with are those who are most needy. Unfortunately, the children who are not the "problem kids," the ones who don't get into trouble, or the ones who aren't as expressive about their needs, are the ones who don't get enough attention.

I have created lunch groups as a way to get to know and spend time with *all* the kids in the school. These groups consist of four children and meet one day a week for a month. At the beginning of each month, I send out invitations that the child tapes to his/her desk. These children get to eat lunch in my office rather than in the lunchroom for one day a week.

Lunch groups are immensely popular. Although I don't have any specific agendas, many interesting conversations develop. The children practice social skills and make friends, and I get to know many more students than I could in any other way. If one of these students later needs to see me for a counseling session, we have already worked toward developing a rapport. I also have many students who have voluntarily met with me after taking part in a lunch group.

I have learned how important it is for me to be genuine when working with children. Just yesterday, a first grader who meets with me regularly said, "You know why I like to come see you?" 'Cause you really like kids!" She's right. I like kids. I put out a lot of energy in my work with them, but it pays off for all of us. Comments like that one are my true compensation for the job I do. The way to teach kids about caring, being honest and having integrity, is to be that way yourself. The children I work with know that I am there for them and that I'm doing my best each day.

Although I work in a school setting, these ideas can be adapted for use by any counselor working with children. If you work in an agency or private setting, try to visit the local school occasionally. Meet with children on their own 'turf' and get involved in community activities, such as recreation centers and after school programs. Use your expertise to present inservices or workshops for educators. Develop a program for children in the community in which you can use your unique skills and abilities. Be creative on your journey to becoming famous.

Being famous is a great opportunity to become an advocate for children. This may not always make you the most popular person with parents, other staff members or your principal or supervisor. There will be times when you have to stick your neck out in order to help a child. I believe that, as counselors of children, this is the most important role we play. We need to be able to stick up for children in situations where they can't do it for themselves. Work closely with community organizations and support politicians who are working towards improving children's lives. Stay current in your counseling organizations and continue to keep abreast of new developments in education and child development.

Last and certainly not least, learn to relax. Sometimes the pressure of the job can be overwhelming and being famous can take its toll. You may find that more demands are made of you, once people learn what you have to give. There can be times when it seems that everyone wants something from you. Setting yourself up to be famous may also mean that you now have a reputation to maintain. Remember that being famous doesn't make you perfect. You don't become exempt from making mistakes or taking a 'wrong turn' once in a while. It's really all about learning, growing and finding your way to becoming the best you can be.

So, you have a waiting list of referrals and there's a mountain of paperwork growing on your desk. You're beginning to feel overwhelmed and you're tempted to put on your shades, sneak out the door and crawl into bed for the rest of the week. It's time to take a break. Go sit in a classroom. Take a walk with one of your students, or play kickball outside at recess. Then, after work, go get a massage! After all, no one said it was going to be easy being famous!

CHAPTER 29

LESS IMPORTANT THAN WE THINK

Diane Blau

A few months ago I retired after devoting almost 20 years to working as a teacher, counselor and family therapist. Coming to this decision was no easy task, for I had learned long ago that it was my role and function in life to be there for my clients as long as they needed me. It was a basic, albeit unspoken, tenet of my core values, much stronger than any urges I might have had to take care of myself.

My decision to retire was precipitated by the realization that I had to introduce more balance into my life. Haltingly I told my colleagues, expecting revulsion, disrespect and challenges that I was abandoning those who needed me most. This, of course, was a projection of my own fear and insecurity. I now know that I had a distorted view of my responsibility and importance as a practitioner. I have realized that my role in clients' lives is not as crucial as I once thought it was.

Since my early days of training and throughout my on-going education in the field, I have been told over and over again what I must do to be successful. Master practitioners extolled the virtues of their respective approaches, and I was exposed to a plethora of books and demonstration videos. At every turn a compelling recommendation, revised formula or new answer promoted the prospect of success. I believed that if I took enough responsibility, studied long enough and worked hard enough, my efforts would meet with success. But my perception of "enough" became distorted, and I began to think I could do more than I could. Finding my way became a matter of great effort. With one child, for example, I found myself engaged in lengthy phone conversations with his third-grade teacher and school principal as well as his parents and grandmother in an attempt to increase their understanding of the child and elucidate their wrongdoings. I was certain that greater involvement would result in more rapid and lasting change. I became the listening ear for everyone's complaints and the resolver of each person's immediate concerns. When called, I rushed to the rescue, armed with interpretations, support and advice. I felt needed and important.

In another case of a couple in marital crisis, I carefully chose each word and intervention as if a single mistake would doom them to eternal misery. Following their initial visits, I consulted a supervisor, numerous colleagues and relevant literature to ensure the implementation of the perfect treatment plan. Again I enjoyed the feeling of power and importance. At times I was even smug in self-appreciation. My ego expanded with each perceived success, and I became skilled in denying or explaining away mistakes and failures. Though the case of the child mentioned above may have gone on longer than necessary and the case of the married couple ended in divorce and an abrupt cessation of counseling, I continued to foster the illusion of self-importance and overemphasize the significance of my role as a counselor.

Even though I became more moderate in my expectations and finding my way became easier throughout the years, when I decided to retire I again confronted my self-perceptions. If I had been so vital in the lives of my clients, how could I leave them? How could they survive without me? What I came to learn, however, was that my clients did manage without me. When I announced my plans, not one screamed about neglect. Newscasters didn't announce "Counselor Abandons Clients." Not one client raced out the door and refused completion of our last months together.

I have come to wonder if others may also have an over-inflated view of their own importance. Finding one's way through the labyrinth of theories, orientations, techniques and practices is, at best, a confusing struggle. Yet being face-to-face with a client in distress demands quick thinking and knowing responses. We grasp for ideas and answers, and in the process convince ourselves that we are right. We begin to attribute too much importance, power and influence to ourselves. We feed our egos and deny our failures. Our colleagues collude in this charade as we eagerly discuss our miracles and cures.

I was struck by this notion of over-importance most recently when presenting a workshop on client suicide to a group of experienced counselors. In the course of a discussion on prevention and risk factors, one counselor boasted, "I haven't lost one yet!" while another said "I've saved more lives than I can count!" These statements ring with assumptions of invincibility. In an advanced training seminar, a counselor spoke proudly of his "ability to shake the clients up and get them moving," while noting their intense emotional reaction as evidence of his success. It was evident to me that if change did occur, it would not be because of, but in spite of his ill-timed and insensitive interventions. Yet his comments were met with nods of approval from his impressed peers.

During these months of reflection I have modified my view of myself as a practitioner. I believe I've influenced many clients. Others I don't think I made any difference with. Some may have even left worse off than when they arrived. Yet to my surprise, I am satisfied with the outcome of my career as a counselor. Not because of accolades or a standing ovation of grateful clients but because I am content to have had a place in the profession.

I have come to believe that we as counselors need a more realistic picture of our role. Yes, it helps to be reliable, responsible and accountable. We need to be well-educated and trained, updated and re-trained. But we need to be aware that each of us alone is potent but not omnipotent.

I encourage new counselors to keep this in mind as they study and gain experience. Develop your own definition of success, one that is seasoned with reason and a realistic perspective, one that takes into account your own humanness as well as that of the client sitting in front of you.

PART VII

TRANSITIONS AND TRANSFORMATIONS

CHAPTER 30

STAGES, AND STAGE FRIGHT, IN THE MAKING OF A COUNSELOR

Garrett J. McAuliffe

Finding your way as a beginning counselor used to be a lot more difficult than it is now. Whereas, in the past, counselors embarked on their professional journey with only a hazy sense of the future, we now have adult development theories to explain regular individual changes which we can expect to experience throughout the life span. This rush to plot general adult development has been no less true for the mapping of the counselor's professional journey.

And, to paraphrase an earlier writer on human development, 'tis a movement devoutly to be wished. As stage theories would have it, we are regularly emerging from a state of lesser to greater awareness, openness and interdependence.

I often wish I had such a map to guide me on the rocky road to my current stage as a counselor. Instead, I plowed through the muck of obscure but fascinating psychodynamicism, the haze of plotless humanism and the well-defined furrow of behaviorism on my way to a more confident "technical eclecticism," as one author recently described one desirable state of counselor peace. Like a quester on the way to Canterbury, or Oz, I poked around with faith, hope and courage through 20 theories, 50 role models, 15 supervisors and 100 conferences to "find my way."

Only in hindsight can I now discern the stage-like pattern of my development as a counselor. So, I offer here the "Not-too-scientific Idiosyncratic McAuliffe Stage Theory" ("NO-ISM") of counselor development, based on an N of one (me). Each stage is accompanied by a characteristic emotion.

Stage One: Innocence or "Tell me exactly what to do." (Typical of us in our first skills course) Emotion: Wonder. Characterized by the "I can't wait for the lesson plan for each client" (I am a former school teacher).

Stage Two: Consternation or "Why aren't they telling me exactly what to do?" Emotion: Consternation and patient waiting.

Stage Three: Simple-minded person-centeredness or "I'll just nod periodically and something will happen. Emotion: None that I'm aware of since I'm trying so hard to listen to *everything* the client is saying.

Stage Four: Imposter. (Occurs at time of first real client or internship) Emotion: Terror. Common thoughts: "I think I'll hide under the desk and maybe she'll go away" or "I hope he's a no-show."

Stage Five: Escape and Fantasy. Emotion: Relief. Common thought: "The client didn't show. So, now what will I do? Maybe I'll try something easier, less nerve-wracking and more structured, like tiger taming for the circus."

Stage Six: Support, Accommodate and Please-the-client or "SAP" stage. (Typical of early internship). Common thought: Be nice, gaze interestedly and look occasionally troubled.

Stage Seven: Surprise. Emotion: Relief. Common thought: "The client returned. Why?"

Stage Eight: True Believer or Fundamentalist Counseling. Emotion: Smug confidence. Common thought: "(Expletive) all this vagueness. I'll be a behaviorist. If I can't see it and count it, it doesn't exist."

Stage Nine: (Our hero gets a job here) *Hero Helper.* Attitude: Hubris. Common thought: "I've got my own office, a salary, a title and a theory. Send me the toughest situations."

Stage Ten: I Could Be Dangerous. Emotion: Pride. Common experience: My mom at a family reunion: "Come see your cousin Danny. He's a bus driver in Brooklyn and he hates it. He's all mixed up." My mom to Cousin Danny's mom, "Garrett's a counselor. Get Danny over here. Garrett can straighten him out. We have a half-an-hour."

Stage Eleven: All Puffed-up and Ready-to-go. Emotion: Fear (again). Common experience: Director: "Here's the new intern. Could you supervise her?" Garrett (doing DeNiro imitation): "Are you talking to me?" (Internal monologue: "Holy ____! I can't do this. Other people supervise!")

Stage Twelve: Existential Angst. Emotion: Enlightened confusion. Common thought: "If some clients benefit from insight, others get helped by behavioral change, still others by reframing cognitions and all by trust and self-acceptance, I'd better rethink my certainties..."

Stage Thirteen: (Many conferences, counseling sessions and supervision encounters later) *The Humble, Ironic Constructivist.* Attitude: Wholehearted tentativeness. Common thought: "I can tune into the client in his or her dilemma, yet maintain awareness of my responses. I can attempt to match an intervention with a particular client issue. I know when I don't know."

And so it goes. This "N of one" has emerged to dwell tentatively in Stage Thirteen, thanks to the heroes of our field—our mentors, writers and caring colleagues. So what use is the No-ism stage theory? It offers no shortcut to "Thirteenness," for one must live it to be it.

Perhaps this theory might serve as a reminder to you as a beginning counselor to remain tentative while being confident enough to act. At some point, you may say, in the words of a genuine stage theorist, "That's how life will be. I must be wholehearted while tentative, fight for my values yet respect others, believe my deepest values yet be ready to learn. I see that I shall be retracing this whole journey over and over, but, I hope, more wisely."

You will perhaps make commitments to counseling theories, client conceptualizations and treatment plans while being open to their potential inadequacy. And, all the while, you'll avoid the "gumption traps" of rigidity, burnout and cynicism. In that sense, developmental stage theories can serve as road maps which might help you to find your way, with a little help from your friends.

CHAPTER 31

FROM PROFESSIONAL GAMBLER TO COUNSELOR

Jay Noricks

I am an anthropologist, professional gambler and student of counseling. Recently, I have been trying to make some sense of these three diverse professions and their connections within my experiences. As an anthropologist, I taught for five years before I was fired for not having completed my dissertation. By the time I did finish my degree, there were few academic positions available. With a family to feed and bills to pay, I found that I was able to develop a latent talent as a professional gambler, most often in high stakes seven card stud.

Currently, I am trying to sort out my gains and losses for a late career in counseling after almost two decades of gambling for a living. Surprisingly, these two career choices have more in common than you might expect.

Poker is a game with very clear rules, extending in a well-run card-room to dealer behavior, and even to where players may sit and how much space they may claim as their own. It is a complete system for interaction. Mathematical or statistical laws determine the best of many alternative courses of action. It is the perfect arena for competitive behavior. It mirrors the external world in the importance of luck of the short term. Long term success requires great patience, discipline, and enormous perseverance. One must be equipped to handle great financial and emotional swings. From the heights of joy produced by outstanding play when combined with the blessings of statistical chance, I plunge to the depths of despair at the apparent punishment by powerful invisible forces that match every calculated move with a loss. While I might make the perfect mathematical moves and predict opponents' hands and behavior with accuracy, I may still lose nearly every hand over an extended period of time. The game requires immense energy and a constant ability to take the long view. To give in to the pleasure or the pain of the moment is to begin to flounder emotionally and to lose the control which brings long term rewards.

The two most important traits a poker player can have are patience and discipline. A year of studying counseling assures me that these same characteristics are also central to becoming a competent counselor. A counselor needs great patience to discover and understand a client's needs and to choose the right moment and the right kind of intervention. Similarly, considerable discipline is required to suppress a counselor's own body aches and pains, to keep the mind from wandering, to maintain attention on a client who rambles on continuously.

There is an essential difference, however, in what I want to accomplish as a poker player versus my goals as a counselor. As a poker player, success means blocking others in the achievement of their goals so that I can achieve mine. As a counselor, success means facilitating others' achievement of their goals so that all of us can meet our needs. There are other differences as well, especially in terms of the respective perspectives or world views of gamblers and counselors.

In order to succeed in the world of poker, I have adopted a specialized perspective which I believe is psychologically unhealthy in the world at large. In the poker room, I avoid personal interactions. While waiting for a game to begin, I usually sit alone, reading. Only occasionally will I chat about wins and losses and the emotional demands of the game with one of the other professionals I respect. But even with these few individuals, as with other players, I want no friendliness to get in the way of my exploiting them to the fullest. I look for weaknesses in playing strategies and flaws in personal character so that I can better use them to my advantage. I coach myself to show no compassion and no mercy. A player in pain is a player who can be more easily manipulated. I find it financially rewarding for some players to dislike me. Some want to beat me so badly that they make mistakes. Even when such a player's bad play is rewarded by the short-term vagaries of chance, I retain a measure of satisfaction in knowing that I have caused him to play badly and I can do so again.

In a conversation with one of my professors I suggested that my skills of manipulation could also be useful as a counselor, except that the manipulation would be for my client's sake rather than my own. He went to considerable lengths to make it clear to me that counselors do not manipulate; they facilitate. I have some difficulty in comprehending the difference, except in the attitude of the counselor and that one's client learns to fulfill his or her own needs in the nurturing environment of the counselor-client relationship. It seems to me that both the counselor and the poker player manipulate certain variables to bring about certain directional changes in others. Call it facilitation if you like, but it still seems to this poker player to be a benign form of manipulation.

Poker allows me to use my analytic abilities in the study of people: regularities, tendencies, emotionality, mathematical skills, traits of stubbornness, enthusiasm, self-doubt, bullying, overconfidence, whining, bragging and so on. It is a game which offers a potential reward for every increment of study. I think the same general statement could be made of counseling.

NEGATIVE VIEW

The environment of a high-stakes poker room is one that reinforces my contextually bound negative view of other human beings. A part of this view derives from the controls I need for continued success, but a part of it is due to the types of people one often meets in a poker room. For example, there are thieves, cheats, con-artists, drug dealers, addicts, loan sharks, deadbeats, railbirds, compulsives, and brokes. In this environment, I am distrustful of people, sometimes slightly paranoid. I am neither generous nor nurturing. I have no compassion or sympathy. I suspect the motives of every individual offering a smile, a handshake or a friendly greeting.

I dislike the displays put on by others and assume that if I was one of my opponents, I would not like me either. I do not like myself in this context, but fortunately I am able to recognize the danger of extending my poker room personality, perceptions and expectations to the external world. I make a conscious effort to assume a different persona elsewhere. I try very hard to keep my poker life separate so that I am able to see the rest of the world with fresher, more innocent eyes. Sometimes I tend toward naivete in my perception of the intentions and motivations of people outside the cardroom, but I see this as a reasonable overcompensation for my experiences as a poker player.

I believe I am a compassionate and caring man, sensitive to the needs of my family, my friends and of other human beings in general. Yet if these are my true characteristics, what do I make of the other me—the one who profits from the manipulation of others, the one who uses his empathy to comprehend the pain of others but chooses to exploit that pain for personal gain rather than facilitate its alleviation? I have consistently tried to separate my poker self from my true self. In fact, I have done so well in splitting off what I perceive as my undesirable self that when I twice took a personality inventory, once for my poker self and once for my true self, three of the five scales (extraversion, openness, and agreeableness) contrasted significantly for my two selves.

Of course, it is a fiction to speak of my two selves. Since beginning the study of counseling I have learned the necessity for a counselor to be totally honest with oneself and of the value of integration of the total personality. Yet, I am reluctant to acknowledge my shadow, to give full value to those aspects of myself which I have treated as my poker self and not my true self for so many years. How am I to achieve and maintain authenticity or achieve intimacy and autonomy if I deny aspects of myself that have played such an important part of my life for 17 years? And what of my tendency to be naive and overly trusting of those I meet in the non-poker world? Wouldn't it be better for me to acknowledge that people are blends of desirable and undesirable qualities, that traits like greed and selfishness are as equally human traits as compassion and generosity?

Isn't this bipolar view of the world a skewed perspective? The poker world is not so negative as I habitually see it, nor is the external world, and especially the academic world, as innocent, supportive and nurturing as I like to perceive it. The greatest benefit I have found so far as I prepare myself to be a helper of others, is that I get to spend so much time at healing myself. This is not an option for me—it is a necessity if I am to find my way as a counselor.

CHAPTER 32

From Musician to Counselor: The Song Remains the Same

Mark R. Gover

Someone once told me that the human body replaces itself every seven years. Within this time, each cell in our body generates, lives, deteriorates and is replaced by a new cell. Thus, in a sense, we are not the same people we were seven years ago.

In the last seven years, I have also become a different person. I have transformed from professional musician to professional counselor, from single person to father and husband, and from baccalaureate to doctoral candidate. Each role requires me to develop in new ways and expand my relating, nurturing and thinking abilities.

These changes have also had deeply intimate consequences. Every now and then I've found my personal compass confused, knocked off balance by the loss of a familiar and stable sense of who and what I represent. At such times I wonder "Where am I in all of this? In the midst of all this change, what personal qualities have stayed the same?"

Perhaps the greatest challenge in any life-change is preserving continuity, an awareness of one's stable and enduring "center." In the midst of changing from musician to counselor, I have often felt like a ship without a port.

Such feelings are understandable; we identify with our careers. From my youth, I had based my self-image on my musical talent. It distinguished me from others and gave me a sense of accomplishment and self-esteem. When asked what I did for a living, "I'm a musician" invariably sparked interest (if not occasional contempt). In fact, I often shared my recordings with people I met—it was a standard part of my introduction. Abandoning such proficiency for a field I knew nothing about was hard, like riding a bike on ice. If I was lucky, every now and then I'd hit a dry spot.

These days the pedaling is much easier. Now I need to recognize those aspects of myself that I've carried forward from my previous career, to integrate music and counseling. What are the similarities between "Mark the musician" and "Mark the counselor?" It's important to examine the constants as well as the losses and gains in transitions.

One aspect that has remained constant in both careers is creativity. As a composer, I often became excited at the first appearance of a new idea (a feeling similar to the proverbial "Aha!" experience in counseling). Later, to arrange that idea, to integrate it into some kind of musical context, was a form of creative play. This experience can be compared to the work (play?) we do as theorists as we mentally arrange the pieces of a client's experience or of various theories into an integrated whole.

Intuition and spontaneity were key aspects of my abilities as a performer. When improvising, for example, I would spontaneously access everything I knew musically and invent or utilize previously learned phrases with the greatest relevance for the moment. Similarly, my work as a counselor provides numerous opportunities to combine old ideas in new ways and spontaneously invent new ones. We can never predict what our clients will present. For this reason, counselors are always improvising to some extent.

Listening to myself was an oft-used musical skill. A musician must learn to develop a critical ear for his or her own performance and incorporate feedback for a *changed* performance. Similarly, I usually can listen objectively to my counseling, hearing both the actual words and the potential in the session.

Along with the ability to listen to myself musically came the need to *work closely with and support others*. As a member of various musical ensembles, I gradually realized that the notes my musical partners played were less important than their belief that they were part of a free, open and accepting musical environment. My objective in counseling is to create the same climate conducive to growth.

My musical training has also taught me the process of *learning a new skill*. Because of this background, I understand that proficiency takes practice and I know what it feels like to improve. Perhaps I had the nerve to tackle a new career because I was comfortable with my inability, having experienced it every time I started to play a new instrument or song.

As a musician, my best compositions and performances were not those that were the most technically complex or sophisticated, but those that were the most meaningful to me. As a counselor, the most meaningful and productive encounters are not usually technically perfect, but show understanding and communication between client and counselor.

There are losses and gains in my career shift. For example, a musician knows immediately if a performance has "hit the mark." In counseling, the effects of an intervention are often delayed, ambiguous or undetectable. I also miss the camaraderie I enjoyed with my fellow musicians. However, I have begun to change and grow in ways I might not have otherwise. I have also had the opportunity to finally indulge my intellectual side, which often made me feel like an outcast among my musical peers.

Prior to my switch to counseling, music provided me with self-expression. I don't play music at all anymore and sometimes wonder, "Have I simply stopped expressing myself? Does an important part of myself now lie dormant and without voice?" Maybe. Or perhaps counseling has taught me that it is impossible *not* to express oneself.

CHAPTER 33

JOURNEY IN A JEEPNEY: A COUNSELOR CROSSES CULTURES

April Peck Herbert

I wind my way past the open fruit market where there are durian and spiny red piles of rambuatan. In the intense morning heat I flag down a jeepney, a colorful "folk art on wheels" vestige of World War II. For the eighth time, I am embarking on a new life in a foreign land. "Kumusta Ka?," the smiling woman next to me asks.

"Ewan Ko." (I don't know.) "Hindi ko naintindihan." (I don't understand.)

Five months have tiptoed silently away since my arrival in Manila, Philippines with my Foreign Service husband, 16-year-old daughter, tiger cat, cocker spaniel, guidebooks and curriculum vitae. I fully intended to be settled in by now, but am daily reminded that cross-cultural confusion abounds in the daily life of this global nomad and itinerant counselor.

I well remember the euphoria and excitement of the initial month. Although there was disappointment that no position in counseling or education awaited me in spite of my experience in high school teaching, college counseling and networking, I was feeling fortunate to have the time and opportunity to explore MacArthur's World War II headquarters on Corregidor Island, to climb the volcano at Lake Taal, and to study Philippine textiles and basketry before building my collection gathered from around the world. Being unemployed also enabled me to care for my daughter who was ill with mononucleosis for one month after arrival and to assist through the trauma of transition from an active high school life in Bolivia to one of uncertainty and ill health in the Philippines. We would talk about exploring the beach at Boracay together, returning to my husband's Peace Corps village of 30 years ago on the island of Mindanao, and of being able to use the professional skills I had worked so hard to acquire during the five years our family was posted back in Washington, D.C.

As the weeks turned into months, the cacophony which is the traffic in Manila blared into my very being. The buses and jeepneys which I had viewed as means of transportation on sightseeing jaunts to Malacanang Palace now irritated me as they arbitrarily stopped for a fare, rarely used brake lights and blinkers, and wove in and out of traffic.

The Filipino way of greeting each other with their eyebrows and a smile became a challenge for me as I was accustomed to greeting others verbally, be it in Spanish, English, Korean, Greek, Indonesian or Irish.

I would remember my rewarding days in La Paz, Bolivia directing a mental health program for the U.S. Embassy and teaching high school English at the American Cooperative School. Now I was an unemployed, frustrated, rootless traveler back at the computer again constructing functional resumes in an unfamiliar foreign metropolis.

During the next stage of my progression to equilibrium came anger. I tucked all the travel books in the lower closets of the book shelf and packed away my files on group facilitation, career development, conflict resolution and mother/daughter issues. Neither the social services department nor the counseling foundation with the newly hired director had responded to my job application and I was growing impatient. I took my advanced diplomas off the wall of the study and packed them in my clothes closet in the bag with scraps of assorted Christmas wrapping paper. I spent all my time at the expatriate club playing tennis and directing my anger about my personal and professional upheaval toward winning the women's tennis tournament. The strategies, determination and fortitude that helped me win this tournament helped me look at the challenge of conquering culture shock as a worthy opponent and was the stimulus that propelled me on to the "live and let live" stage of cross-cultural adjustment.

I started driving again, in spite of the traffic congestion and lack of familiar rules. I stayed along a relatively straight path with imagined lanes as my guide, driving defensively and occasionally leaning on my horn. A game I invented helps me appreciate the 350,000 jeepneys which ply the streets of metro Manila. I laugh at the names of these vehicles painted in bold, acrylic colors across the top to the windshields. Names such as "Dark Justice," "Road Star," "Fatal Blows," and "Economics of Love" have me creating Stephen King-like sagas as I maneuver through the traffic. I once again want to learn about the culture in which I am living. An exhibit featuring the culture and arts of Philippine minority groups, such as Ifugao and Kalinga will count me among its attendees in the upcoming weeks.

With time and a modified perspective, I have become more open to both cross-cultural and career opportunities. Might I be approaching the approval stage of cross-cultural adjustment? The loss of the comfort of our home in South America overlooking the Andes and the resignation from the job teaching literature left me vulnerable for a time. As the security of a familiar role was shed, I needed some time to recover from the jolt. Although I have acculturated numerous times before in distant directions around the globe, I am awed by my own and my clients' powerful feelings associated with loss, international relocation and rebuilding.

As I sit here tonight across the Pacific in my new home in Southeast Asia preparing for a meal of chicken adobo cooked with vinegar, pepper and garlic; bangus, a herring-size fish lightly grilled; and balut, a half-broiled, ready to hatch duck egg (you can distinguish the beak and the feathers), I am certain that cross-cultural readjustment is a richer, fuller experience than any textbook has dared serve its readers.

As a sojourner abroad, daily conducting an exploration of cultural identity, I think of the counselors in the rapidly changing rural and urban areas of the United States who find themselves increasingly working with the culturally different. Perhaps some or many are struggling with a way to make these counselor client relationships more effective. With attempts to more gracefully find my way through the cross-cultural maze in the Philippines, I find focusing on my own personal cultural identity to be helpful. What specifically are my own ideas about family structure, roles of individual members, interpersonal interactions, rules of behavior and discipline, religious beliefs, perceptions of time and space and life expectations? Where are there gulfs with my host country's cultural beliefs and what is my action plan for recognizing commonalities and building understanding during my stay?

If I am able to recognize the alteration in my sense of self during the cross-cultural transition, perhaps I will be better equipped to facilitate my clients' process of integration into a culture not their own.

Perhaps soon, amidst the piles of jackfruit, durian and spiny red piles of rambuatan I will say: "Naintindihan ko. Salamat" (I understand. Thank you.) Perhaps soon, following difficult work in the United States, you will hear the same phrase softly spoken.

CHAPTER 34

WHERE DO I GO FROM HERE?

Deborah Linnell

That warm May afternoon more than a decade ago looms vividly in my mind as if it were yesterday. As I put on my police uniform in preparation for the evening shift, I smiled, reflecting on how four years ago to the day I had entered the police academy to become one of only twenty women in a force of 932 men. I was proud of my chosen career and I was finally beginning to feel comfortable in my role. I was beginning to gain acceptance by my male peers, little by little, step by agonizing step. It had taken a lot of hard work to get this far, especially after my pregnancy and maternity leave more than a year before. It had been the "ultimate female thing to do," but it was worth it. I was on my way to settling down in a way that I had never dreamed possible.

There wasn't a cloud in the sky that day as I kissed my daughter goodbye. She followed her usual ritual of taking down my waist-length hair and trying to make me look more like her mommy than a police officer set on defending the world against all evil. I looked at my watch as I rushed to the car and put my hair up again.

The evening shift started with the usual array of calls for domestic violence, car accidents, and a sexual assault; nothing out of the ordinary. As the day darkened into night, my next call was to investigate a suspicious vehicle, involving the driver's ex-girlfriend. As I approached the address, a rose-colored Cadillac matching the description of the suspect vehicle pulled recklessly onto the main road. The erratic driving suggested that the driver was intoxicated and that I would probably end up making a drunk driving arrest. "Maybe the guy will stay in jail long enough for things to cool off between them," I muttered under my breath as I approached the car.

I suddenly felt that sixth sense that told me something was terribly wrong. While the driver acted intoxicated when he got out of his car, leaving the door open with the engine running, something just didn't seem right although I couldn't seem to pinpoint it right away. As he reached into the car, he said, seriously, "Officer, I've got something for you." My heart stopped as a shiny object flashed a few inches away and my survival training took over. During the struggle, I was pulled into the car and felt the back of my head press hard against the steering wheel and my face was suffocated by his chest. My forehead made sharp contact with a shoulder holster and my chin rested against the small handgun in his waistband. I felt the gear change on top of my head and then he pressed the accelerator to the floor. For what seemed like an eternity, I felt my legs dragging outside the car, desperately struggling for a breath. I fought back and found myself flying into the path of on-coming traffic on the darkened roadway, slamming onto the pavement at what was later estimated to have been in excess of seventy miles per hour. I could barely move my finger to press the radio button to call for help. Instinctively, lying face-down in the street, I followed police procedure and gave the dispatcher a lookout for the vehicle and driver while people around me screamed at the horror of what they had just witnessed.

Later in the emergency room, the real pain, the terror of what had happened, hit me full force. I was a police officer and had a job to do, I wasn't supposed to feel such emotional turmoil. How could I show my emotions and risk being criticized by my male counterparts? The police psychologist came and went in the crowd of other officials, staying just long enough to make sure that I would live. I could barely think straight and the detectives started wondering aloud if my head injury was more serious than first thought. After more sedation to dull the physical pain, my little girl, carried by her daddy, was allowed in to see me. The initial news reports had said that I was presumed dead so they didn't know what to expect. The moment when our eyes met is when the true pain hit. I can still see the horror in her face and hear her scream as she saw her mommy attached to tubes and unable to move. My bloodied arm laid on top of the sheet, the same arm she loved to snuggle against as we got ready for storytime. *Her* arm, she called it. My terrified baby girl clung to her daddy and cried and I could do nothing to comfort her. I just laid there helplessly, crying inside.

Twelve agonizing days later I was released from the trauma center but returned to the hospital periodically for more surgery. I was anxious and frightened about returning to work, not knowing if I would be blamed for getting injured. The doctors kept telling me I would be going back to work by the end of the month, then the end of the next month, and so on. I was still having trouble walking, was in excruciating pain, and couldn't see straight; but, they were the experts, I had to trust them. Each specialist had their own diagnosis and preferred medication and physical therapy regimen and I found it difficult to get any one of them to see me as a whole person instead of as just a collection of body parts. I kept getting more and more depressed and began considering, and then planning, my suicide on a regular basis. I no longer trusted my ability to make rational decisions.

Several months after my injury, my daughter and I entered a local grocery store. I quickly identified with the drawing in the meat department of the cow labeled as parts of beef. I had difficulty walking and a woman I didn't know yelled at me for being "drunk" around such an adorable little girl. My heart was broken and my spirit wasn't far behind as I vowed to limit my public contact as much as possible. I started walking close to walls and learned to run my finger along a line in the wallpaper's design to maintain my balance. I couldn't walk across the room without falling, so I learned to stay along the fringes. I worked hard to hide my imperfections and was ashamed to see people I knew.

Then, nearly a year after the incident occurred, my career was suddenly over. I was told that I was being retired on disability based on a neurologist's report of extensive head injuries that would only worsen with time. I was devastated. I didn't know what to do and I wanted to die. I now had to redefine my self-image. I would no longer be the police officer that my daughter could be proud of, rather I would be forever a damaged person who would never recover. How could I protect my little girl from the evils of the world when I couldn't even protect myself?

After the retirement was official, my treatment regimen changed dramatically, although I was still going to about a dozen doctor and physical therapy appointments every week. Instead of an optimistic prognosis and rehabilitation planning, the appointments became a series of "limitation listings" and I quickly learned all the expenses not covered by Worker's Compensation. I was told everything that I would never be able to do again, both physically and as mandated by receiving a police disability pension, and no one seemed to have any suggestions about what I could do. I felt even less like a person and more like a lifeless robot.

I wanted to find a way to continue at least part of my life plan. I had many more intense periods of depression as I tried to figure out a way to salvage what was left of my life. I wanted to finish my education and go on to graduate school so that I could help people in another way than I had originally been trained. My therapist explained that his job was to protect the profession from "unfit people" and that I should consider law school instead because they had "allowed several handicapped people in that field." I quickly learned the private agony one suffers by having physical limitations.

The head injuries and high doses of multiple medications affected my ability to read and write so my daughter and I spent many hours watching Sesame Street. She patiently listened as I tried to read every children's book I could get my hands on. Except for my daughter, I didn't have a single person who thought it was possible to complete a college degree, but I had to try. I just couldn't sit at home and become a breathing vegetable. My daughter deserved a better role model than that.

Attending class after getting injured was terrifying. Faculty members found it difficult to talk with me without staring at my casts or crutches. I patiently listened to the various descriptions of their reactions to hearing about me on the evening news and fearing that I had been killed. Funny, though, no one seemed interested in how I felt about what was happening in my life. It was like I was expected to reassure them that everything was fine and I had to be very careful about who knew the actual extent of my physical and cognitive limitations.

I enrolled in a college study skills class and was fortunate to meet the director of the university's learning center. I needed someone to have faith in me *and* who was willing to help me with the struggle. He believed that I had the right to achieve as much as I wanted to achieve. I developed a new set of problem-solving skills along with re-learning the basic academic skills and he encouraged me to find a counselor who would listen to my inner struggles without judging me. It was a long, difficult process, but I finally found another safe place.

Throughout my struggle, my study and work with others has become focused on how people cope with the long-term effects of violent crime. Through my recovery process I have learned two important lessons that directly apply to the work we do in the helping professions. First, it is crucial to see people as whole persons rather than in the isolated parts they are able to share with us during brief visits. Our clients should never have to feel like the parts of beef in the grocery store drawing. It is important for the various disciplines to work together as a team, rather than having territorial restrictions, to assist those in the greatest pain. Secondly, coping with the recovery process needs to be addressed directly as an issue. Bouncing from one specialist and physical therapist to another, being interviewed by the police, and testifying in court can be just as difficult, if not more so, as the initial trauma and it is very easy to become repeatedly traumatized by those who are designated as helpers.

So, now I'm left with my original question, "Where do I go from here?" I am still struggling to find my way as a counselor. I need to incorporate my prior experience and training rather than to deny its existence. I want to train helping professionals across the varied disciplines to work with people as they face the struggles of long-term traumatic life events.

CHAPTER 35

MORE THAN MY REFLECTION LOOKING BACK FROM THE MIRROR

Alan W. Forrest

Within all endings are the seeds for new beginnings. Knowing this does not make the endings any less difficult or painful. Even those endings that I initiated have presented me with challenges, but my clients have graciously given me gifts of understanding.

I recently left the private practice where I worked for the last five years. Although I was excited and enthusiastic about my new job, I was also ambivalent about what I was leaving behind. As a counselor I was aware of the therapeutic significance of the termination process, but usually I would concentrate on the client's reactions to the impending loss of the relationship. As I prepared to terminate a caseload of clients, the emotions struck me with a force that I could not have imagined.

"Letting go" is an essential part of the counseling process. The way in which closure is addressed and dealt with determines whether clients leave with or without an increased sense of their own inner resources and the ability to manage future difficulties. Termination, an important experience for clients, may be when the counselor influences clients the most. There is potential for enhanced growth and resolution.

I had told my clients months earlier that I planned to leave, but now it was time for them to develop new relationships with other counselors and continue treatment or leave counseling altogether. I was aware of all the interpersonal dynamics that could swirl around the minds of the clients: some would feel abandoned and manifest that as anger, a recapitulation of prior losses; others might put up a wall to hide their hurt, sadness and pain. How could I make my departure into a healthy therapeutic lesson on life's cycle of endings and the potential for new beginnings? How would I deal with my own sense of loss with the clients that I had made a professional and emotional commitment to assist?

I believe that each of our experiences adds to a tapestry of our lives. Each life event enriches and fills in the gaps with depth, sensitivity and understanding about who we are and who we will become.

I feel fortunate in having selected a career that focuses on relationships, for I believe that life has no meaning if we don't connect with others. By connecting with my clients I have learned more about myself.

I have one client who is my age—statistically, we are at the midpoint of our lives. We both wrestle to understand who we are and how to navigate in a world that is both exciting and mysterious. We are naive and idealistic enough to wish for a world of understanding and acceptance. But my client has AIDS and his future is not as boundless as mine. His time is limited. He has taught me that AIDS is more than a disease that happens to other people. He is a sensitive, caring and loving person. I have learned again of the importance of looking beyond the labels we attach to those who seem different from us. I have learned that when I look into a mirror there is more than my own reflection looking back.

Since I was a college student, I have struggled with my spirituality and the part it plays in my everyday life. I perceive myself as an empiricist, grounded in the scientific method, studying that which is both observable and measurable. But I reflect on another client, with a strong belief in her "Higher Power," who has resolved her existential and spiritual questions. She is at peace with her spirituality, but the issues she brought to therapy were more personal; how to live and communicate with and love her husband, how to not expect herself to be perfect and her lifelong battle with her weight. Throughout these struggles, her spirituality never waivered, even though, while I saw her, both her parents died and her husband was accused of child molestation. I learned from her the serenity that comes with acceptance and the belief that there is more to life than what we can observe.

As I closed the final file and packed up the last box I realized that I needed to review and grieve for my time as a counselor in private practice. It was a wonderful adventure filled with many successes and failures. Maybe I had made a difference to some of those that placed their trust in me and maybe I could have been better with others. I had heard many secrets, some that needed to be remembered, many that needed to be forgotten. Memories can be prisons or containers of warmth. Thanks to my clients, my memories are rich and warm. All of the hugs, all the goodbyes, all the genuine caring and best wishes only served to accentuate what I was leaving behind. But I was also taking them with me. All of my clients that freely and not so freely contributed to my tapestry were coming along for the ride.

The upcoming chapter of my life will be built on the collected knowledge of what came before it. Somehow, through the goodbye tears, that thought gave me some solace.

CHAPTER 36

MEETING THE CHALLENGES OF A LATE-BLOOMING CAREER IN COUNSELING

Kathy Potter

Sometimes I find it amazing that at age 49, I am still finding my way, but when I realize that I came to the counseling professions only a few short years ago, I am more understanding of my uncertainties and false turns. I am writing this piece for those of you who, like myself, had 'other lives' before we discovered our inclination for and skill in, counseling others.

Although I was an English major in my "first life," I also studied philosophy and was interested in learning more about myself, "the meaning of life," and the path(s) to greater enlightenment. I was not a natural-born counseling type, nor did I grow up in a particularly dysfunctional family. My early years were not permeated by thoughts of saving the world or unlocking the answers to why people behave as they do. I enjoyed, what I consider, a "normal" childhood.

When I got older, I raised two sons, first as a married person and then as a single parent. I also worked to earn sufficient income and chose to go back to school to become more marketable in the business world. The struggle of those years resulted in two secure and loving sons, a master's degree in human resource management, management experience in a corporate setting and the increased awareness that I wanted to be on my own and doing something that was closer to the person I was becoming. Yet, who was I at this middle stage? For me and many others at mid-life, the question of self-identity becomes of paramount interest and I decided it was time to go back to school.

I know I am not alone. So many of my classmates, and perhaps many readers, went through a similar transition at this mid-stage in life. In my graduate counseling program, there were many fellow students who were reassessing their careers and life choices: homemakers with grown children who wanted to use their well-developed listening and empathic skills with others; teachers who were burned out in the classroom and needed to transfer their caring and knowledge of students to another arena; ministers who craved a way to bring spirituality and counseling skills to a wider audience than their individual churches allowed; retired persons who felt a need to give back to society in a personal way; and business persons who experienced a meaninglessness in their professions and needed to do something they considered helpful to other people.

Going back to school was a terrific experience; however, after recently receiving my counseling degree, I am facing dilemmas that push me to the limit. As part of my pre-counseling-degree life, I did outplacement consulting, so I am acutely aware of the difficulties—and rewards—of career changes. What I was not as prepared for was the frustration of having enormously useful life experiences, but not the years of clinical or direct counseling experience that employers want. When I applied for licensure, as I attempt to start private practice or when I consider contributing to the various professional counseling organizations to which I belong in the way of hands-on experience or research efforts, I feel an often overwhelming lack of competency, an inability to have an impact in a field where I finally feel at home.

In addition, because I did not specialize in a specific area, such as addictions counseling, treatment of sexual abuse survivors or family systems therapy, I do not fit into the positions available in the job market. In career consulting, we caution our clients to be flexible and willing to learn new skills to meet the constantly changing workforce needs, but in the field of counseling, we seem to be demanding more and more specialization. Arguments, pro and con, can be made for this emphasis, but the dilemma for the older returning student or practitioner in counseling is that specialization takes more time and money and forces us to close off parts of ourselves that are valuable for helping clients.

In looking for a job, one of the strongest emotions I feel is fear. Fear that I won't be able to use the skills I've developed in a setting that supports both my emotional and financial needs. In this part of the country, social workers are in great demand and the MSW is the ticket of admission to clinical positions as well as most other counseling-related jobs. Should I have pursued the MSW even though that degree didn't fit me? From a pragmatic viewpoint, the question still haunts me, usually at around 3:00 a.m.

To help diminish these fears and questionings, I frequently remind myself that I have returned 'home' at an older age, with different financial and ego needs than I had at age 20 or 30. My new 'family' is composed of sisters and brothers who have already produced material, provided services and promoted the field and themselves for more years than I have. Changing my expectations of how much I can contribute helps me cope as does the belief that 'when one door closes, another opens.' I know that my frustration and self-doubt are endemic to all persons who change careers.

As I reflect on my situation, I ask myself several questions: What are ways we later-bloomers can participate in the profession that are beneficial both to ourselves and the field without starting at the bottom with salaries that cannot support the needs of older adults? How can academic institutions that offer counseling programs be more responsive to the increasing numbers of older adults who are returning to school and require career considerations different from traditional-age, master's-level students? In what ways can we older adults contribute to the profession and achieve recognition at a time in our lives when most people have already reached certain levels of acceptance and professional acknowledgment? Several partial answers occur to me.

In the area of institutional support for returning adult counseling students, I have several thoughts: Perhaps schools should advise aspiring students who don't have certain backgrounds, about the pitfalls of entering the profession later in life. This suggestion goes against my beliefs about career changes, but it may be necessary. Schools should help establish mentoring relationships between students and non-faculty, practicing counselors so that students can get first-hand information on what counseling is really about. Students should be informed and encouraged by all professors to join the national and local organizations that are specifically related to the students' interests and disciplines. And schools should establish on-going, long-term relationships with institutions and organizations that can provide evening/weekend hours with supervision for working adults trying to fulfill their internship requirements.

Although I can't possibly enumerate all the ways our social organizations could change to accommodate older adults re-entering the counseling profession, I can make a few suggestions: Hiring institutions in the counseling field should find ways to become better informed about the gifts mature adults bring to a workplace even if the exact specialty is absent. Adults are adept at learning and our broad-based experience often is more helpful when working with a diverse population than is a narrow specialization. In addition, organizations can re-examine their experience requirements for positions to see if there are ways in which life experiences, as well as or in place of paid professional counseling experience, can be assessed for potential contributions. And finally, in-

159

stitutions need to pay better salaries across the board for counseling services and employees.

Adult students also have opportunities to help themselves. Students could establish peer support groups with the schools providing assistance through speakers, occupational information, career center services and creative ideas for the groups. In addition, late-blooming counselors need to accept that their desire for recognition, monetary rewards and significant professional contributions may not be met to the extent they would like. We must possess clear understanding that whatever contributions we make, they are valuable to ourselves and to others regardless of the quantity or lack of our life-long professional involvement. Who knows what impact occurs from one article, one presentation, several counseling sessions or even one empathic statement to a distraught individual?

I feel I am now at that place one writer spoke of where what you do not know is the only thing you know. I am eagerly and yet anxiously searching for the right soil in which I can grow and contribute to the world around me. We older counselors may be late-bloomers, but often our flowers are sweeter and fuller and provide more depth to the gardens we brighten.

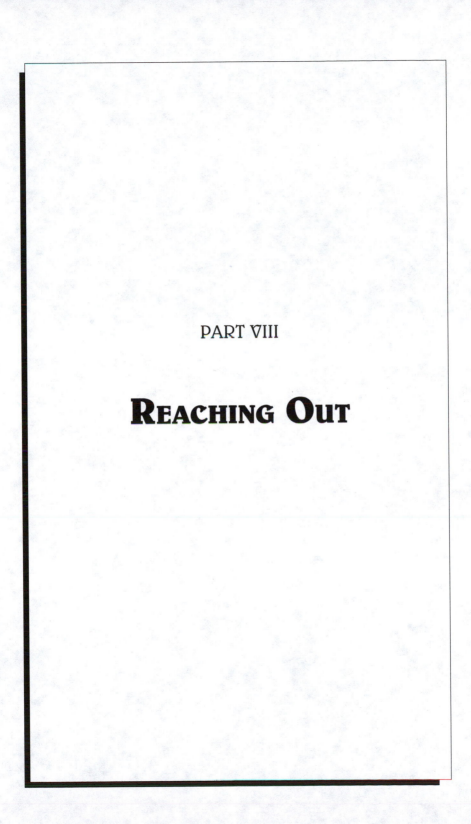

PART VIII

REACHING OUT

CHAPTER 37

ALONE IN THE DARK

Jeffrey A. Kottler

Like most people who gravitated to the counseling profession, I thought I was entering a "social" discipline. Because the profession's roots are in education and the social sciences, and because it focuses on inter-personal communication, I believed counseling would provide not only a career but a family. I began my training with great excitement.

I have always felt like an outsider. When I became a counselor, I thought I was joining an exclusive club of dedicated professionals. I was prepared to learn the secret handshake and code words. I attended all the appropriate meetings and conventions. I worked as a team player. I tried to find jobs that would give me opportunities for social engage-ment and intellectual growth.

Since counselors are, by and large, a gregarious bunch, I believed that, by joining the profession, I would find my way out of a life-long shell of shyness. I would become part of a larger community of people who shared similar values, interests and aspirations. No longer would I have to find my way alone in the dark; I was in the company of others with whom I could hold hands.

Little did I realize what a solitary form of work I had chosen. I quickly learned that, though I worked in the company of others, I rarely had time to talk to them. We were always busy doing things that seemed so important. When we were together, most of our time was spent "being productive" or fighting for our individual agendas. The lack of sharing and supportiveness bothered me, and quick hugs or superficial "How's it goings?" only made me more frustrated.

So, I retreated into my cave. Now, I sit in my office, seeing a stream of people who come in to tell their stories and seek relief. Their lives are often interesting and sometimes excruciatingly painful. I listen. I do my best to respond helpfully. And I keep everything to myself. As a counselor, I am alone not only with my own fears and inadequacies, but with everyone else's as well.

If, as a beginner, I had understood the extent to which my essential aloneness would be intensified in the counseling profession, I would have become a farmer or truck driver. I never realized that counselors have so little time to be with and help one another. The clock is always running. There are clients to see, meetings to attend, paperwork to catch up on, phone calls to return.

"Sure, I'd love to chat with you, but I really have to finish this project."

"How's it going? Really? Sorry, but I have a client waiting."

"You're having a tough day? Wait, I have to take this call."

Must we become clients to get some attention?

After many years of practice, I realize that I have profited from all the solitary reflection I have done, but it was my clients and students who helped me find my way through the dark, not my colleagues.

I recently returned from a trip to New Zealand, where I visited a number of agencies and counselor education programs. I was astonished to witness enactment of a cultural institution that I had read about but never experienced firsthand: teatime. Every morning at 10:30 and every afternoon at 3:00, everything comes to a halt. Secretaries stop answering the phones. Staff members cease whatever they are doing. Everyone wanders down the hall for a break. No one talks of work; people sit around and talk about rugby, politics, books, movies, their children.

Everyone I know who visits New Zealand (or other Anglicized nations) falls in love with this custom. We tried it in our college, but faculty members just walked in at the chosen time, grabbed doughnuts and coffee, and then went back to their offices to work. Who has time to sit and chat?

The conventions of our practice prevent interruptions. Once in a session, we are cut off from friends, family and the rest of the world. We are prohibited from discussing what we do, except during designated moments. Sometimes, we are so busy juggling our various roles and responsibilities that we hardly notice that night has fallen outside or that we are "in the dark" with a client, unsure of what is happening.

We may become unsure of what direction to head in or how to deal with obstacles in our careers. Clients cling to us, pleading that we shed some light on their own paths. Supervisors tell us to move faster. Sometimes, it feels as if we're going around in circles and that we may never find our way.

Stop. Spend time with friends and colleagues. Have a cup of tea.

Reach out to your colleagues for the recognition and support you so richly deserve.

CHAPTER 38

REACH OUT AND
TOUCH SOMEONE

Jesse Brinson

As I reflect on my growth and development in the counseling profession, I liken my experience to the maturing of an infant growing into adulthood. When I catapulted out of the womb of graduate school into my first counseling position, it seemed as if I spent much of my time babbling, drooling, crawling and falling on my rear end.

Still wet behind the ears and suffering the after-effects of that traumatic birth experience, I longed for the support and nurturing of a trusted confidant to help me adjust to this new and exciting profession. This guidance became increasingly necessary for me the more I realized that my graduate experience had not prepared me for the "political" dimensions of the profession.

It took several years before I stumbled upon someone to help me diffuse some of the stress I was experiencing. In other words, I found a person to help me find my way through the political maze that seemed to encompass, at least from my vantage point, a significant portion of professional counselors' daily experiences. This individual not only became a trusted friend and confidant, but a mentor who helped me develop professionally.

Obviously, anyone who is just starting out in a profession would value the support of individuals who lend their knowledge and expertise toward helping him or her achieve success. While this was certainly true in my situation, I did, however, approach this relationship with a degree of skepticism. Although there was nothing about the behavior or attitude of the individual that gave me reason for pause, the fact that he was a member of a different ethnic group presented a dilemma for me. Since the historical relationship between our ethnic groups has been strained, I was inclined to ask myself, "Why is this person interested in seeing me succeed?" Yet, through spending time and getting to know him as a person, I eventually rid myself of the stereotypes that otherwise would have made it impossible to foster a productive mentoring relationship.

Having a mentor made a world of difference in my growth as a professional counselor and educator. Not only did I find someone who could provide me with the wisdom, knowledge and experience of many years in the profession, but I found someone who was willing to serve as an advocate on my behalf when I faced certain crossroads in my career.

I also found someone to confide in about my fears and concerns of being a novice in the profession, without feeling as if I would be judged as incompetent. This was important for me considering the profession of counseling appears to be primarily an individual enterprise in which we spend so much of our time alone with our clients. This situation tends to create an "every person for him/herself" perspective in the hearts and souls of many practicing professionals. Having a mentor protected me against potentially harmful stressors of the profession and the unfortunate reality of many school, agency and university settings where there actually are people out there to get you. As a result of my mentor's support, I became more creative and productive in my professional endeavors. I improved my self-confidence and self-esteem and have established a number of professional contacts.

I am grateful for several other ways in which my mentor helped me, especially during times of professional and personal crises when I felt discouraged and dispirited. It made all the difference to have someone in my corner.

Other counselors were not as supportive or encouraging. It sometimes felt like I had been marked for failure and that, in their minds, I was not good enough to fit into their "elitist" world. One day I went to check my mail and found someone had placed job announcements from other work settings in my mailbox, positions that were specifically directed to minority professionals such as myself. It was difficult, but knowing that others were supporting me made it easier to confront the individual I believed had done this.

Years later, I now share my experiences with you in hopes of reaching other beginning professionals who are trying to find their way and don't know where to turn. As counselors, we should look for ways to help each other succeed. As someone who has been in a number of mentoring relationships, I am willing to pass this spirit along to others in need. I strongly encourage other counselors to seek someone they can trust to act as their mentor. Here are three important considerations when selecting a mentor:

1. Identify individuals in your work environment you most admire and most easily gravitate toward.
2. Limit the extent to which you let race, ethnic background and gender influence your decision. Although it is initially more difficult to develop trust, crossing racial boundaries has strengthened my social consciousness to curtail distorted perceptions of others.
3. Select a mentor with a proven track record. If the individual has a history of mentoring other counselors and appears to be genuinely concerned about you as a person, then this is the type of individual you want behind you.

In the final analysis, as one of my professors once said, "In order to succeed at anything in life, you will always need the help of others." A mentor can be an invaluable resource in helping beginning counselors reach professional success. Reach out and touch someone.

CHAPTER 39

BEING YOUR OWN MENTOR

Jeffrey A. Kottler

Reaching out to a mentor, someone more experienced than you are, is certainly critical to finding your way as a developing professional. There are limits, however, to what others can do, or are willing to do. The realities of many work settings is that there is just not the time or opportunity to have as much supervision and guidance as you would ideally like. Often we are left on our own to figure out things as best we can.

I just finished teaching a "Theories of Counseling" class and I realized for the first time that it is really more about history than contemporary practice. There was a time when each of us affiliated closely with a particular theoretical model, cheerfully calling ourselves behaviorists, existentialists, gestalt, rational-emotive or client-centered counselors. We joined forces with others who felt the same, read the new research and innovations related to our "school" and worked to become even more proficient in the application of our particular model.

I don't know the exact moment I realized that the profession has evolved to the point that we no longer identify with one theory, practicing it dutifully, regardless of the client's preferences, issues and clinical situation. But there I was, presenting the various theories to beginners in the field, as if they should pick one and expect to stay with it for their lifetime.

Once upon a time, that was the case. In our uncertainty and panic over how to do this complicated job, we enthusiastically embraced a model, *any* model (although hopefully one compatible with our basic beliefs about people), and then reveled in the comfort of knowing that we belonged somewhere. There was no special handshake, but there certainly was a feeling of camaraderie among those of us who read the same material, attended the same programs and supported one another in the belief that we had chosen correctly, while others were clearly misinformed.

In today's world, however, new counselors begin jobs with the idea that they may indeed find their way in the profession by choosing a particular theory as a "home." (After all, they were instructed by someone like me who told them that this was a good thing to do.) The difference is that the demands of contemporary practice and the open exchange of ideas among professions and practitioners make single-theory allegiance virtually obsolete.

Is there anyone practicing today who does not value the therapeutic relationship, systemic thinking, cognitive interventions, role playing, modeling or task facilitation as modes of operation? The melting of artificial boundaries, the integration of diverse models, the identification of universal core ingredients in all helping systems, is leading to an epistemology that is a synthesis of what is known across disciplines and theories. "What theory do you follow?" is now an irrelevant question. Treating individual models as if they were practiced in "pure" form is now obsolete.

So what should new practitioners do to find their own way in the field? Studying theoretical models as *history* is certainly useful to find what is common and universal among approaches. Experimenting with different theories is helpful to narrow the choices to those most compatible with your clinical setting, client needs, personality and preferences. More than anything else, we should all work to:

1) combine the best features of all theories,
2) integrate the latest research into current practice,
3) transcend the artificial boundaries of disciplines,
4) exchange ideas more flexibly with professionals who think differently from ourselves, and
5) find what drives "good" counseling, regardless of the concepts, terms or language used to describe those processes.

Finding our way in the profession means thinking for ourselves. This search involves the work of synthesis, not exclusion; of flexibility, not rigidity. It means responding to each client's requirements based not on the theoretical models alone, but on the client's best interests. There are times when relationship-oriented or task-oriented work is preferred, or the clients need to be supported or confronted. At other times the focus is legitimately placed on thoughts, feelings or behavior, or individual, group or family modalities are preferred. Sometimes the emphasis should be on content or process, insight or action, the past or the present.

The reason that there are few professionals left who use a single theoretical model is that most of us now realize that clients require different things from us, depending on their presenting complaints, their interpersonal style, their cultural/ethnic/gender background, their unique perceptions and the dynamics between us. A client manifesting "borderline" features, or one who is chronically abusing alcohol, clearly demands a different treatment than one recovering from divorce or struggling with AIDS. Perhaps there are some theoretical models encompassing and flexible enough to be universally applied (certainly their authors claim that is so). I suggest that even if we operate from a consistent set of philosophical assumptions that are organized as a guiding theoretical structure, this model cannot be called by anything but YOUR name. Nobody else counsels quite like you do. The variability within each school of thought is just as diverse as it is between different models.

Finding your way as a professional may have begun with the choice of a particular theoretical model. Many of us may still identify with these conceptual assumptions. But one of the consequences of experience in the field is that we continue to learn alternative ways to function. As we adopt these ideas for our own purposes and integrate them into our clinical style, we alter forever our theoretical approach.

Studying various theories gave us the historical and conceptual foundation to formulate our own beliefs about how and why people change. With every class we take, workshop or convention program we attend, supervision session or conference we experience, with every book we read, conversation we have with colleagues and certainly every counseling session we conduct, we change the way we think about our work and how we will operate in the future.

The time has come to stop trying to be exactly like our mentors, imitating as closely as possible the way they work, following their models as if they were written in stone. Finding our way as counselors involves pursuing each of the themes discussed within this book—dealing with our own personal issues, confronting ourselves, listening to our clients and what they have to teach us, following their lead, responding to their unique needs. It is critical, as well, that we reach out to others for support. Yet, ultimately, in finding our way in this profession we must not only reach out to others but also reach inward to ourselves. When we can use a conceptual framework that reflects consensual opinion about research, theory, practice and ethical standards, and one that still embodies what is unique to each of us, then and only then can we find our own way—and help each client to do the same.

The voices of the counselors you heard throughout this book spoke about their attempts to find their way in this profession. The authors spoke honestly, sincerely, and courageously about their fears and joys, their hopes and nightmares, in the hope that their stories might inspire you to dig more deeply into your own professional and personal life.

There is no job more difficult than the one that we do. Feeling lost comes with the territory. We spend hours every day in the company of others who are suffering, who are manipulative, and who pressure us for answers that we don't have. Yet being a counselor gives us permission, if not the mandate, to keep searching to find our way. It is through this courageous journey that we inspire our clients to follow our lead, to face that which we all fear the most.